For

The Mag[ic]
music live on!

~ Heahe[r]

SOME KIND OF MAGIC

LIVIN' THE RHYTHM OF COMMUNITY DRUMMING

BY

HEATHER LARSON POYNER

authorHOUSE™

1663 LIBERTY DRIVE, SUITE 200
BLOOMINGTON, INDIANA 47403
(800) 839-8640
WWW.AUTHORHOUSE.COM

First published by AuthorHouse 10/24/05

ISBN: 1-4208-5909-9 (sc)

Printed in the United States of America
Bloomington, Indiana

This book is printed on acid-free paper.

COPYRIGHT AND PERMISSIONS

The following authors and publishers have generously given permission to use excerpts from copyrighted works. From The Healing Wisdom of Africa, ©1998, Malidoma Patrice Somé. Reprinted by permission of the author. From Drum Circle Spirit, by Arthur Hull, ©1998. Reprinted by permission from White Cliffs Media, www. whitecliffsmedia.com. From Drumming to the Edge of Magic, by Mickey Hart and Jay Stevens ©1990. Reprinted by permission from 360 Productions and Mickey Hart. From the compact disk, Songs of the Spirit, ©1996, Barry Bernstein. Reprinted with permission from Barry Bernstein.

***Some Kind of Magic** is dedicated
to my dad, Read Larson, an artist with
unparalleled passion for the written word.
This is for the man who always said to me:
"I hope you're writing this all down."*

*And for:
My teachers, mentors and muses—drumming, spiritual and
otherwise—
(Instead of long, boring Acknowledgements, you get Chapters 8
and 9!)*

Table of Contents

Foreword ix

Prologue xi

Chapter 1
In the Beginning...1

Chapter 2
Quantum Reading 5

Chapter 3
Drum Call...11

Chapter 4
Two hands, three notes...15

Chapter 5
The Barry Experience 23

Chapter 6
Opening our Doors: Rhythm in the Round 29

Chapter 7
Stepping into the Circle 39

Chapter 8
Teachers, Mentors & Spirit Guides..53

Chapter 9
Full Circle: Our Extended Family of Rhythm 59

Chapter 10
Worlds of Facilitation 65

Chapter 11
Do Try This At Home—And Everywhere Else! 75

Chapter 12
Trust the Song..81

Chapter 13
Not Just for Kids, Not Just Drums..87

Chapter 14
    Recognizing Our Worth 95
Chapter 15
    Magic, Magic, Everywhere..103
Epilogue 111

Foreword

When I first met Heather Poyner, I was publicly sharing something that I myself was just beginning to understand: Drums speak directly to something inside of people—no need to go through the brain first. That rhythm is an ancient catalyst with the power to unite, excite, empower and heal. Witnessing the effect drumming had on Heather helped me more deeply understand its potential and to refine my intentions and methods to share the message.

Many individuals and organizations devote valuable resources to promoting and cultivating a sense of unity within their communities. This can often be an elusive goal, as messages tailored for one faction of the community don't always resonate with others. The challenge of transcending age, ethnic, social and economic boundaries becomes a goal worthy of all attempts.

Heather's book is a wonderful collection of observations, lessons learned and personal responses that came from her journey into drumming and ultimately, her path to becoming a rhythm facilitator. Right from the start, Heather responded to the call of drums from a place she did not fully understand. It was as if the call was in a language that she had yet to learn, though the underlying message came through loud and clear.

The book employs Heather's communication skills, an inherent fascination with the world around her, and a willingness to share her views while inviting others' interpretations. Believing all along that if it could happen to her, then others too were likely to respond, Heather opened first her heart, and then her home, so that others would feel comfortable responding to the call of the drums.

There is no road map or guideline for such a journey. The process of exploring yields the clues and guideposts as needed—often at unexpected times. Going further on any path often includes inner exploration as well. What started as a pleasant personal discovery for Heather quickly transformed into a calling with universal implications. Responding as she did has had a profound effect on hers and others' lives.

There are several good books heralding drum circles as healthy, healing activities good for building community. And many others with "how to" information. All are valuable. This book humanizes Heather's role of facilitator as her skills, confidence and conviction grow concurrently with the expanding reach of the message she shares with others. Having faced similar challenges and rewards on my own path, I enjoyed her book as both testament and guidebook.

We all stand on the shoulders of giants. For rhythm facilitators, this includes Babatunde Olatunji, Arthur Hull, Barry Bernstein, Mickey Hart and Christine Stevens. These pioneers helped create and nurture a healthy rhythm community with a far-reaching welcoming message: Together we can raise awareness and understanding of this effective medium for building community. Their efforts in teaching and mentoring others have expanded the realm of rhythm facilitators, and continue to provide guidance and support.

While this book celebrates the success of her journey, Heather doesn't avoid sharing the obstacles and struggles along the way—self-doubt, public misperceptions and naysayers. She also honors the many elements that help any venture become a success: support and inspiration from family, friends both new and old, teachers, strangers and an ever developing trust in her own intuitive nature—the very source of her initial response that has proved both valid and true.

While sharing Heather's personal journey and growth, you may find parallels to your own journey as well. The material translates well to non-drumming situations. Anyone who recognizes that group energy can be enhanced by a caring presence, and willingness to accept responsibility, will find much to enhance their own path.

In the years since we met, I've stood beside Heather as a colleague, sat in her circles helping hold the beat, commiserated over the challenges and celebrated with incredible awe this amazing community that we are so privileged to work with and be a part of.

Rhythm has drawn us in and it is rhythm that empowers us to assume some level of responsibility to share what we believe in. Heather's book, as well as her life passion, is "Livin' the Rhythm" and that she offers both in full view of her community makes them all the more resplendent.

Thank you Heather for sharing, in so many ways,

—Tom Gill,
Rhythm For Unity

Prologue

Have you ever walked by the beach or through a park and seen a group of people playing drums with their hands? Did you maybe put a little more distance between yourself and that group because you thought they must be "a bunch of crazy hippies?"

Or maybe you thought there was something interesting about that music and those folks but they still seemed a little too different. "That kind of music" is known as community drumming—a social activity in which people of all ages and abilities come together to sit in a circle to create improvised music with instruments ranging from African drums to plastic buckets. Originating with indigenous peoples throughout the world thousands of years ago, community drumming has re-emerged in Western society in recent decades. Many people are participating in community drumming today because the drum circle offers a place of accessible creativity and trust in a world that is increasingly short of such commodities.

This book is about "this kind of music" and "these kind of people" from the viewpoint of someone who, after five years, is still amazed and delighted by all of its aspects. This book does not trace the rise of drum circle culture in this country. Instead, its focus is on the immediate impact group drumming has had on my life and the community where I live in southeastern Wisconsin. It records about where I've been, what I've done and whom I've come to know. Just as importantly, it is about lessons I've learned along the way and how "I" has become "we" in the process.

To present this journey I draw on personal journals, diaries and even notes made during telephone conversations. These materials come from a lifelong habit of journaling, and the "occupational hazard" of 14 years as a newspaper reporter.

Writing began when I received my first "Daily Diary" bound in cream-colored faux leather with a little lock and key as a birthday gift at age 11. As I religiously penned the seemingly news-breaking details of my pre-teen existence, I became addicted to the act of writing and perhaps, a bit infatuated with my own words. By the next year I told my mother I would be a writer when I grew up. What it would take to get to that place were chapters yet unwritten, of course.

In the 36 years since that declaration, a stockpile of diaries, notebooks and scraps of paper have recorded "life's great truths" as I have seen them and more often, anguish over the less-than-great moments. Like my brother and sister scribblers, I often pondered the possibility of producing a book, to the point of outlining full-blown book concepts (four to date). This, however, is the first time I have set sights on seeing one through from conception to birth.

From the beginning, this book has been different from the pre-books that have preceded it. Its concept, title, start date and deadline all hit me at once, after a single phone call. On Aug. 16 2004, I had a conversation with a woman I had never met about the possibility of doing a drum program with a group of developmentally disabled adults. It was not anything she specifically said, but something in the tone of her voice that told me what I was doing with drums, what *we* do with drums in a circle, has a particular quality that *is* magic.

I was inspired to write this book as soon as I hung up the phone. Within 24 hours I also had a deadline—the book's birthdate, so to speak. My father, to whom this book is dedicated, would turn 80 years old on June 10, 2005 and I knew I would have a manuscript to present him on that day. I also knew that it would take a month to clean up and print out, which meant that this manuscript would need to be "good to go" by May 16, 2005—exactly nine months since the magic began.

This chronicle begins—like most of my work—inscribed in a wide-ruled spiral notebook with a black ballpoint pen that happened to be lying around at the time. Of course by the time anyone reads it (including kind friends whom I will ask to look it over), this book will have been transcribed to word processor, floppy disks, electronic editors and all manner of high-tech word-massaging software programs. (Curiously, it will also have had a near-death experience when the author first tries to input it into said cyber-technology.)

The book's genesis is significant because, as the writer Marhall McLuhan observed, "the medium is the message." In my case, writing in a spiral-bound notebook is a reflection of *my* personal medium and message—low tech. I prefer making bread without a bread-making machine, I choose a wooden spoon over a food processor and for recreation I ride a 1974 three-speed Schwinn bicycle. And, as already noted, these first 36 years of writing have not been on laptop computer, but in diaries, notebooks, on cocktail napkins and on the occasional matchbook cover.

My choice of low-tech is not from obstinacy or fear of the new and unknown. It is, rather, out of respect for what some call "the Source." This Source is the original form of energy, intention and spirit of a given action. To me there is something vital, if not sacred, about staying close to the Source. Gadgets, e-mail and even grocery stores can diminish this vitality. Instead of visiting friends on front porches, we zap off electronic notes—but can we really replace the sound of that friend's voice with keystrokes on a computer screen? We forget that the bread begins by nurturing yeast to bloom; the birthday cake is but a delicate dance of moist and dry ingredients; and that the satisfying journey by the lakefront comes from the simple action of muscle energy against pedals driving a chain and two wheels.

This is a view of Source that relates to *my* experience. Other cultures view Source from a perspective that works for them. For some, the Source of things transcends everyday experience and, paradoxically, even the need for written language.

In his book *The Healing Wisdom of Africa*, Malidoma Patrice Somé writes of how the people of his West African village view Source:

> The Source of all, the Dagura believe, has no word. It has no word because meaning is produced instantly, like a cosmic and timeless awareness. So to the Dagura, there is an understood hierarchy of consciousness. The elements of nature, especially the trees and plants, are the most intelligent beings because they do not need words to communicate. They live closer to the meaning behind language…Wise men and women in the indigenous world argue that humans are cursed by the language they possess, or that possesses them. Language, they insist, is an instrument of distance from meaning…At the Source, words would not be necessary, for meaning would be produced instantly.

As a lifelong writer my personal challenge is to walk this line; my challenge to put into words concepts I have come to believe transcend words. This struggle, for me, is where Source meets Magic. For those of us hopelessly—or hopefully—hooked on sharing our insights with the rest of the human race, Somé offers this eloquent encouragement:

> The good news is that using language also
> means that we are on our way back home,
> journeying to the source of meaning.
> Those who can't stand being trapped in
> a place where language tends to distort
> move into poetry, chant, rhythm, and
> ritual to speed up their journey home.

Source and Magic are focal points of this book, so it is appropriate that this book about a journey with hand drums begins in a spiral notebook with a ballpoint pen. Because in hand drumming you cannot forget the Source—you ARE the Source!

This is my journey with a no-tech instrument: hand drums—drums and hands, it doesn't get much more basic than this. No large-scale note scales to commit to memory; no multi-stringed instrument attached to an electronic box with buttons and toggle switches. Just me, my hands and a drum. And me, my drum and *other people* and *their* drums and hands, making incredible music *together*, no experience necessary.

And there's more—of course there's more: the subtitle of this book, that "community" thing. That I link *my* journey to community is not a lightly considered detail. From my first conversation about a hand drum I saw the drum as a doorway to something more. I heard that this low-tech hand drum was the instrument used to explore a way of relating to other people—in a circle of music makers defined not by their expertise but by their willingness to explore their own creativity.

Drum circles seemed to offer a new paradigm for community. Here was a space where individuals could discover how to transcend differences in skin color, sexual orientation or so-called musical ability. I wanted in on this place of connection, this place of magic.

If a prologue's purpose is to present a book's reason for being, then I declare that this work begins with the intention of chronicling the steps along my personal drum path. But long before I turn in pen for word processor, I recognize that this is not my book or my story. Drumming in community has shown me that I am not a showman or performer, I am a facilitator. As such I am irrevocably called to be as much a part of the circle as to stand in its center.

I also acknowledge that I am not alone in what I do or why I do it. Throughout the nation and in the Midwest there are many who walk this path and from whom I have learned about the way of the drum circle. To name a few would leave out too many. Those who I mention have walked most closely with me on this journey.

Who should read this book? Anyone who has witnessed or taken part in a drum circle; anyone considering convening a drum gathering in their own community; anyone who feels moved by rhythm even if, and especially if, they don't know why. It is the intention of *Some Kind of Magic* to celebrate an amazing and evolving journey—and the knowledge that we're going there together.

Chapter 1

In the Beginning

...There was a dark basement in a church building on the west side of Milwaukee.

...There were 50-plus people of all ages, some sitting in pews pulled into a circle, some standing, some dancing and most all playing some sort of percussion instrument.

...There were Native American-style drums, drums with goatskin heads, Tibetan bells and seedpod rattles...

But most of all, in the beginning, there was this *music*. A roomful of sound—percussive and melodic; a hum of instruments vibrating and bodies moving—all connected through a song that had never been written.

And I was part of this song. I was not a symphony-attending-witness of the world premier of some new opus. I, who could not decipher the code of written music, was playing upon a borrowed African drum, helping create this never-before-heard musical masterpiece with dozens of people I had never met.

The time was 6 a.m. on Jan. 1, 2000. The event was one of many unique celebrations designed to usher in the eve and first day of the new millennium. It was titled "DRUM 2000 World Wide Synchronized Drum Circle." The epicenter of this event was Taos, New Mexico; its genesis was with an organization called All One Tribe Drum. Local versions of this worldwide event were coordinated by hand drummers and musicians throughout the country. The plan was for drummers around the world to create song when each of their respective time zones reached midnight on Dec. 31 1999.

This event came to my attention via a newsletter for hand drummers called *Hands On Drumming*, edited by a Milwaukee hand drummer and teacher named Tom Gill. How I became connected to Tom is the topic of another chapter, but suffice it to say, something really grabbed me in one of the articles in this newsletter.

The advantage of being lifelong packrat allows me to quote from the newsletter saved from that time. The notice read:

Taos, New Mexico: To All My Relations **YOU** are the one to make peace happen. It's not too late to join or organize a DRUM 2000 World Wide Synchronized Drum Circle for the Millennium. When all time zones have reached midnight, people across the planet, together will drum, pray and meditate on the heart rhythm for one hour. In the USA this time is 7 a.m. (Eastern Standard Time)—6 a.m. Milwaukee—Jan. 1, 2000. Picture it, at the beginning of the millennium, hundreds of thousands of people sharing one prayer and one rhythm simultaneously. How better to seed our good intention for the next century.

Reading this newsletter in a bubble bath sometime in December 1999, I knew I was in. I didn't ask why, but knew I liked the sound of a "heart rhythm" and knew I had to be there doing something—I didn't know what—with a group of people I had never met. I knew it had something to do with celebrating and looking forward, and I wanted to be part of that.

I started out by celebrating New Year's Eve at midnight with my family in Kenosha, Wisconsin. I went to bed and awoke at 4 a.m. to leave the house at 5 a.m. so I could be in Milwaukee by 6 a.m. on New Year's Day.

I arrived a few minutes before six and found my way to the basement of St. Ann's Church. In the dim light I found a spot on a pew and took my drum, borrowed from Tom Gill, from its bag. A song of sorts was in progress, a harmony of diverse sounds with a vibrant, underlying pulse. A man who I later learned was named Elijah Paul, garbed in a suede tunic with beads and feathers and holding a tribal-looking staff, was leading a chant. Several women in Middle Eastern dance attire shimmied to the beat playing small cymbals strapped to their fingers. I touched the spotted goatskin head of my drum and felt it vibrate to the rhythms in the air. Not caring that I had never played before, my hands joined the drumhead and I entered into the song.

But wait there's more—In the Beginning...there was also a Sunrise.

After we officially welcomed in the last time zone—7 a.m. Milwaukee time—several people decided to drive over to the Lake Michigan shoreline to see if we could catch the sunrise. We packed up, piled into a few cars and drove quickly east. Those in our vehicle realized that the sunrise was imminent so we landed at the first lakefront spot and grabbed up our instruments. As we began to play, the red-orange sun rose over the gray-blue horizon and we greeted the new day of the new millennium.

For the next two hours we beat upon drums, clanged bells and clacked sticks and even "blessed" a tree by tapping musical plastic tubes against its bark. At one point a man walking by the shoreline broke into a verse of an African song I later learned was "Fanga," a song of peace and welcome from Liberia.

After a coffee shop breakfast, our hearty and hardy band disbanded. I loaded the African drum into my van, telling Tom I was not sure if I was ready to purchase it yet. Graciously, he said he'd let me think about it a while longer. It didn't take me long. The magic and the music of the day caught up to me as soon as I hit the southbound on-ramp to Kenosha. I realized that something had shifted for me; something very big and very important. Speaking out loud I said, "I don't know what this is going to be, but I need this drum in my life. I am going to call Tom today to tell him I am buying this drum. I will name the drum 'Millie' in honor of the new millennium."

Chapter 2

Quantum Reading

Before the Beginning there was another beginning—the point of departure that led me to that dark basement full of magic-filled music. My call to group drumming may have seemed to come during an enlightened moment at 11 a.m. on Jan. 1, 2000, but it was actually the culmination of many years of deep thinking and truth seeking. My path to the drum was paved with New Age readings and mid-life questions like, "Why am I here?"

It is not surprising that I *thought* about drums long before I actually heard or touched one. This is because I come from a long line of people who look at life from the inside out. From the first time I heard the word "introspective" in poetry class freshman year in high school I knew it related to my outlook on things. From that point on whenever I wanted to understand something about the world—from the nature of God to how to buy a car—I did my homework, consulting known authorities on the subject first (the Bible, the *I-Ching*, *Consumer Reports*).

Life events such as dating, marriage, children and careers sometimes put other passions on the sidelines, and I stopped reading for a couple decades to attend to the business end of living. A shift along the way brought me back to the books, which in turn lit the way to the drum.

The shift began in 1996 when I was 39, mother to Lauren and Alex, wife to Roger and part-time reporter for the daily newspaper in Kenosha, Wisconsin. After six years of creative and satisfying journalism I found myself moved to a no-man's land of press release rewrites and one-line announcements for church bingo and spaghetti dinner fundraisers.

Shortly after re-assignment, I began to experience unexplainable aches and pains. My right shoulder froze to the point where I could no longer lift a gallon of milk; I had a string of daily headaches that lasted for six weeks. Standard medical testing and treatment did not improve things.

Having given modern medicine a shot, I looked to alternative methods for curing ailments. These alternatives were the low-tech techniques by which civilizations had cured their people centuries before the advent of CAT scans and stomach-oscopies. I explored curative methods of Traditional Chinese Medicine (TCM) including acupuncture and qigong (like Tai Chi but even mellower) with positive results.

As my physical being rebounded, my spirit called out for more. Voraciously I began to read again—one title leading to the next until I got the message that physical existence is undeniably interconnected to spirit.

Previous to this time, I had dabbled in spiritual speculation; mostly along the lines of mainstream religious thought. Although acquainted with the concepts of Zen Buddhism and haiku poetry (chiefly through my father's business travels and personal library), I did not embrace a particularly alternative mindset. My parents had both been artists with bohemian leanings but I had grown to be a fairly cautious and conservative adult.

Rediscovering reading after nearly two decades I began to delve into books of the soul-searching, body-healing variety. My new reading list included: *Back Pain: Chinese Qigong for Healing and Prevention*, *Zen Catholicism*, *The Saviors of God*, *The Tao of Jung*, *The Three Pillars of Zen* and some of the writings of reincarnation guru Edgar Cayce. This took place from 1996 to 1999—a span of three years, significant to me because important things in my life always come in three-year increments.

I also began to encounter the work of writers of the so-called New Age genre—modern thinkers who choose to revisit ancient wisdom, such as James Redfield author of *The Celestine Vision* and Gary Zukav, *The Seat of the Soul*. Two books that had the most impact were Deepak Chopra's *Quantum Healing* and *Called by Name* by Robert Furey.

Quantum Healing suggested some interesting, new-to-me vocabulary and as yet unexplored-by-me new worldviews. Three ideas that grabbed me from this book:

- A river is both always the same and always changing.
- Our bodies are also both the same and constantly renewed. Since our birth each of our cells has died and been replaced several times over. Still, there is something that continues on, making "us" always "us."
- The underlying principle of quantum theory that presents the simple but eloquent notion that the atomic particles that make up everything are but a tiny percent solid matter held together by a vast expanse of energized space. (That the *connections between* the particles are what really make things happen in the world.)

Continuity and change; space and energy; death and renewal: not exactly exotic or headline news, but each serving as a catalyst for change that was imminent in my own life.

I read *Called by Name* in 1998 with a book group at St. Andrew's, the Episcopal church in Kenosha we attended. The book's premise was that by listening carefully and paying close attention, we will discover our purpose in life—our true calling.

It seemed everything I was reading contained words like: "callings," "awareness," "synchronicity" and "convergence" and, of course, "coincidence." I began to examine my career as a journalist as a calling with a particular mission. In a personal journal entry of March 3, 1998 I wrote:

> Blending Furey's insights with those illuminated by Gary Green (the priest at St. Andrew's) a pattern emerges—a validation of my personal quest or style. My calling is to connect the disconnected. My (newspaper) career allows me to write connections—introduce one group of people to another group of people or things to which they can connect.

I enjoyed touching people's lives through the written word, but I was getting restless for a new vehicle of connection. Early in 1999, I began to explore new directions for my "calling." My experience with massage therapy and body/energy work such as qigong, led me to briefly entertain the idea of becoming a hands-on healer of some type.

Yet, for reasons that had as much to do with paying the bills as anything else, I continued to work for the newspaper. By 1999, things were not too bad—I was again writing lifestyle features and a weekly column on the topic of food—but "the time's they were a'changin' " as were duly noted in my writings of that time:

> I see my role as moving energy along—passing it along, keeping it flowing. To do this I cannot hang onto the energy myself; it can do

7

no good to others if it stays locked
within me. To effectively act thus,
I must become and remain a clear
channel...

Author's Journal,
Feb. 21-23, 1999

My recent back injury, (a seemingly insignificant event of pulled muscles) I realize was sent to jump-start my journey as a "seer-seeker, helper-healer." What I don't know yet is what part—or if all—of that is where I will direct my given energies. The job at hand is to discover, cultivate and *set free* those energies so others can be helped and nourished.

By autumn of 1999 these winds of change took on a "drum theme." Within a span of three months I came into contact with ethnic drums three times: through a newsletter, a program presented at my daughter's school and in the pages of a mail order catalogue.

Sorting through the mail at work one day in September, I noticed a newsletter called *Wayra Cholla* ("the winds of change"), edited by a man claiming to be a Western-trained medical doctor and modern shaman in Gurnee, Illinois. The newsletter mentioned a lecture on Western shamanism that had recently taken place at a medical facility in Kenosha (unnoticed or unrecorded by Kenosha and its media at the time).

Rather than tossing the newsletter, I read about Richard Sandore's journey from obstetrics physician to spiritual guide for vision seekers in Machu Pichu, Peru. Although I was pretty sure I wasn't signing up for the Peru expedition any time soon, I was intrigued enough to order an audio tape titled *Introduction to the Sacred Shamanic Journey*. For some reason I specifically selected the version that offered an entire side of something called "shamanic drumming."

One afternoon sometime in October, my daughter came home from middle school and announced that the students had been part of an unusual program that day. "This man came in with all these drums and jumped around a lot. We all got to play them and he had more energy than the gym teacher!" Lauren exclaimed.

In early November I had a freak accident that necessitated emergency surgery for a hernia repair. It occurred while rehabbing an apartment at commercial property we owned. (Lesson learned: It is *not* a good idea to scrub a filthy kitchen for eight hours and *then* decide to tear up carpeting

8

glued to a linoleum floor.)

Sandore's audiotape arrived two days before my surgery. Reading the liner notes I learned the intention of the shaman's journey is to lead a person through a meditative process. Aided by drums, rattles and shakers, the traveler goes to a place where he or she contacts animals of the spirit world for guidance in the "real" world. Figuring that I might be in a place of discomfort (and mind-altering painkillers) I decided to save the tape to listen to during my recovery.

My first dose of drumming was thus heard in the context of healing myself. I don't recall contacting my spirit animal (although images of soaring on the back of an eagle come to mind), but I do recall the steady drumbeat, the universal heartbeat rhythm, and the continuous hum of a shaker-rattle in the background. It was not an instant cure, but the sounds made my journey to wellness a good deal more pleasant.

Finally, while sitting around getting better, I happened across a holiday gift catalogue offering New Age treasures such as Bali-print sarongs and jade Buddha incense holders. Flipping through, a picture of a hand drum caught my eye. It was goblet-shaped with inlaid mother-of-pearl and had some kind of skin tied to the top of it. I found myself oddly drawn to the photograph. I wondered what this drum would sound like, or how the drumhead would feel under my hands. The picture of the drum seemed to embody something I was looking for, something that had been coming towards me for a long time. I realized I had been hearing about and been affected by drums a lot recently and now it was time to have one in my life.

The drum was only $64 (plus shipping and handling) but my *Consumer Reports* mindset told me to be cautious of buying something that might not be a good value for the money. I felt that buying a drum was a spiritually significant purchase and I was not about to get something that would be a disappointment when it arrived.

I set the catalogue aside, but not my desire to purchase a drum. I remembered Lauren's school program and "the man with the drums." If I were going to buy a real drum, I should talk to a real person about drums, I thought.

By now I could almost hear drumbeats in my ears. When Lauren could not remember the man's name, I threw common sense and good manners aside and phoned her teacher at her home on Thanksgiving weekend, 1999. Judy (who was kind enough not to express annoyance for being phoned during a well-deserved break) said she thought it was "a Bill something" and that she would find his name and number when they returned to school.

I was pretty eager to get that phone number. I didn't know it then, but I was moving closer and quicker towards something I penned on March 17, 1998:

> When we think/feel a calling we
> begin to experience connections
> to it in the world around us. Like a
> new sense; perception; new focus
> to old lenses...
>
> Application is the next, crucial
> step. We can't just sit around and
> "groove to the calling." It's the
> "Where do I go from here?"

Chapter 3

Drum Call

> A "drum call" punctuates the beginning
> of any rhythm circle. It is the opening of
> the event, the forming of the relationship
> between the circle and the facilitator,
> defining the beginning relationship
> between the circle and all the parts of
> itself.
>
> —Arthur Hull,
> *Drum Circle Spirit*

On Dec. 7, 1999, I took the phone number given to me by Lauren's teacher and called "the guy with the drums," Tom Gill, of Milwaukee. I told him how I had heard about him and said I was interested in getting a drum. I asked if he could give me pointers on finding a good quality one.

Looking back, I am not sure if I got a definite answer to "how to find a good drum" but in the hour we talked I became sure that this "drum thing" was something I needed to pursue. Although I had phoned for information from him, it became obvious that the sharing was a two-way street.

Tom told of how he had been "drawn to the drum for its own magnetism." In the past five years he had gone from a traditional job to teaching hand drumming, conducting programs like the one he had presented at Lauren's school and hosting informal music sessions at his home.

We discovered similarities in books we had been reading and, in the New Age-type language of the day, it seemed as if there was a synchronicity of our life paths. Looking at the word "synchronicity" from a language point of view, it is interesting to note that "syn" comes from the Greek for "same" or "together" and "chronos" means "time." Thus people or events that are "synchronistic" are "in the same time." Drumming, I was about to discover, has an energy that can indeed bring people together who are "in like time."

In the course of conversation, I also discovered this drumming thing was not "just about a drum." It seemed this drum also came with groups of people of all ages getting together to experiment with a different kind of music.

Tom's response to my question of how to select a good hand drum was to advise me to try a few first. He gave me names of music stores in Milwaukee where authentic ethnic drums were sold. He also invited me to try the drums at events called "drum circles." He noted that he hosted drum circles twice a month at his house adding, "There's a circle coming up this Thursday."

As we closed the call, I thanked Tom for his time and all of the information. As to the invitation to drop by the next drum circle, I was pretty sure I wasn't going to drive to Milwaukee to play an unfamiliar instrument with a group of people I had never met. The spark of curiosity may have been struck, but I was comfortable in my "wait-and-see" zone.

A few days after that conversation I received a small package addressed with unfamiliar handwriting. Enclosed was a cassette tape of music created at the drum circle I had not attended. Tom had added an introduction in which he said he thought I should hear what this music sounded like, to "feed my desire to engage with drumming."

Immediately following his words, there was the sound of a large gong being struck—the vibrations of which lasted a full 30 seconds. Then: a patter of drums of various pitches, gradually gaining in volume and tempo along with a mix of percussive instruments. The instruments came together in song but not all the same song; rhythms switched yet stayed together as if the players were held together by invisible musical threads. A tapestry of sound was being woven with plastic items, a glass bottle struck like a bell, and the galloping beat of drums. Occasionally a voice called out: "Hey you're pretty good on that!" or "Is that your drum?" The song ended with a thundering drum roll and at least one person exclaiming, "Wow!"

This, the first drum circle song I had ever heard, lasted 10 minutes. Listening to the tape nearly five years later, I am able to pick out the voices of people (Tom, Len, Sandy, MJ, Michael, Bonnee Beth) who have since become friends. Even after sitting in and leading many circles since that time, that song marks a special place in time for me. In this first "drum circle dose," I didn't just hear "great music," I heard "great energy."

This music and this energy were new to me, yet the appeal was a strange familiarity. I didn't realize it at the time, but the drum circle songs I heard on Tom's cassette tape were a response to a call I had put out a long time ago. On Feb. 24 1999, ten months before hearing this tape, I wrote in my journal:

> Beyond Words
> The experience of being in and of
> the moment and every moment that
> has ever been or will be.
> Finding the Rhythm of the
> Universe.
> The true intention,
> Yours and beyond you,
> You and as you are part of
> everything else.
> Dissolution of dualism.
> Zen.
> "Ah ha" that hits you like a gong—
> or maybe just the reverberations of
> its sound
> Not the stone, but the whirlpool

I had been looking for "the Rhythm of the Universe" and the Universe sent me the drum. I had heard a gong in my soul and Tom sent me a tape of its voice.

Not long after I engaged with community drumming I learned from Tom and Arthur Hull the term "drum call" refers to the first song of any given drum circle event. It is the part of the program in which players meet their instruments and one another and together they develop a kind of "musical trust" that leads to amazing in-the-moment music. By spending time with me on that first conversation and following it up with a live recording of "the drum circle thing," Tom, the rhythm facilitator, had facilitated my first steps towards community drumming.

Now THAT's what I call a Drum Call!

Drum circle facilitator Tom Gill, who welcomed me to the world of hand drumming in 1999.

Chapter 4

Two hands, three notes

Tom's invitation to the drum circle and the sample of drum circle music did indeed "feed my interest to engage with the drum." The circle sounded like a place where all comers were not just accepted but invited and encouraged to participate. The drum circle tape heightened my desire to get my hands on a real drum. After investigating some of the stores Tom had recommended, I decided to see what he had in stock. On Dec. 19, 1999, I met Tom and the drum that I would soon christen "Millie."

Tom did not just try to sell me one of his drums but said I should get a drum that suited me. Among the types of ethnic hand drums he introduced that day was a style known as the *djembe*, (pronounced gem-bay), from West Africa. Tom explained that its goblet-shaped body was carved from African hardwood known as dembu. He demonstrated how to find three notes, called "tones," on the drum and a couple rhythms using two of the notes. For someone with no formal musical training this looked like something manageable. It also looked like fun.

Of the two djembes I saw that day I was drawn to one that had a cream-colored goatskin head with a pattern of brown spots. When I hesitated to purchase it right then and there, Tom offered to let me borrow the drum for a while to see if it was a good match for me. Surprisingly, I think for both of us, no money was exchanged that day. Tom's decision to let me borrow this $235-drum was based on trust—not just trust that I would bring back or pay for the drum, but some intuition that I was about to make a connection worth far more than the cost of any drum. Grateful to be entrusted with such a beautiful thing, I went home determined to give the drum my full consideration.

Back at home I began to "devour" my new gifts—the wooden drum, its beautiful carrying bag and printouts of the rhythms Tom had demonstrated. I also read through the newsletter that told me about the New Year's Day World Wide Millennium Drum. Although I had not been ready to attend a drum circle when Tom first suggested it, these things fired me up enough to decide to take the borrowed drum and play it in that dark church basement on New Year's Day.

At this point it is important to introduce the members of my domestic circle who graciously allowed me to pursue this new passion—my family. When I first arrived home with the drum, reaction from Roger, Alex and Lauren was fairly mild. They seemed to think, "Oh, OK, its just Mom, coming home with a large drum in a burlap bag that says 'Africa Alive.' No big deal." It became a bigger deal, however, after my "drum epiphany" by the lake on Jan. 1, 2000, when every day I began to try to actually create rhythms on my new drum. For anyone who has not had to share a house with a large African drum, try to imagine your relative peace and quiet punctuated by intermittent reverberations sounding mostly like *Boom Boom Boom Bah Bah!*

Not being selfish by nature, I was acutely aware that my new hobby was: 1) loud 2) not necessarily something my family wanted to hear. As it was dead winter in Wisconsin, I did not have the option to take my instrument to the nearby lakefront or other park spaces in town. One late afternoon in January, I was practicing "Mama Pappa" which sounds a little like *Boom Boom Bah Bah!*, when I heard Roger return from work. His thoughts, as I could pretty much guess, were along the lines of "I don't think I can take much more of Heather and that drum."

I met him at the door to say that I realized this was really loud and would try to figure out how to practice without disturbing everyone. One possible option would have been to go to Milwaukee to play with drummers there. That night, or a few nights later, the situation resolved itself: Roger asked if he could play Millie. Turning on the stereo, Roger, who hadn't touched a hand drum before, began to play an improvised percussion accompaniment to the music of Santana. For the Poyners, hand drumming had just become a family affair.

"If you can't beat 'em, beat the drum!" Roger gets on board with hand drumming, seen here playing his first djembe.

For my part, I needed another dose of the drum circle. In mid-January, 2000, the only person holding drum circles within a 60-mile radius that I knew of was Tom. Despite an aversion to driving at night with an ice-frosted windshield, I drove to Wauwatosa on the third Thursday of that month. Even as I made the last turn on the highway I hesitated, worried that I knew nearly nothing about how to play my new djembe. But, thinking this could be an important evening, I kept on driving, denying the urge to turn around and go home.

In the basement of Tom's home, a group of 14 folks were all playing, all seemingly quite comfortable with jumping into the song of the moment on instruments ranging from African drums to ridged plastic cups scraped with bamboo chopsticks. I immediately liked this atmosphere of acceptance, but soon things got challenging. Someone suggested we work on parts to an African song ("Fanga"). The pace accelerated and pressure to keep up made me feel stressed.

On the drive home from the circle, several things went through my mind: I thoroughly enjoyed being part of a group of people making music together; I was committed to the drum as my primary instrument; and I now realized the drum came with a certain set of complexities.

As an instrument, the African djembe's appeal was its accessibility. By the time I met Millie I had already attempted standard note reading at least three times in my life (if we don't count elementary school music class). I figured if I hadn't broken the code by then (age 42) it wasn't meant to be. From what I could tell, this hand drum had three basic notes and I had two hands—when compared to the daunting dynamics of instruments like pianos and violins, the drum won on math alone!

That said, it doesn't mean that Millie and I immediately lived happily ever after. In fact, the comparison of my journey to your basic fairy tale is quite apropos. To get to what I perceived as the goodness of community drumming, I had to first wade through a few swamps of self-doubt and do battle with energy-draining vampires cleverly disguised as my day job and domestic obligations. Still, this would be a pretty sad fairy tale if these challenges were not eventually met with a lion's share of triumphant moments and a king's ransom of reward.

Like anyone who embarks upon an important quest, I started out with great confidence. In fact, before my first drum lesson, I dubbed myself with the e-mail name "djembelady" (spelled "djembelade" because the other spelling had been taken by another drummer out there in cyberspace).

Shortly after my first drum circle experience, however, confidence became tinged with the realization that the drum was more challenging than I had at first thought. Intuitively I felt the djembe was accessible, but intellectually I had doubts about being able to master the complex rhythms of a culture that was really not mine. My e-mail name, djembelade, now seemed at best wishful thinking and at worst, a cocky overestimation of my innate ability.

Vowing to connect to some solid drum instruction as soon as possible, I first looked to what might be available in my own backyard. I figured that the arts community might be a good place to start and contacted Kathy Ross, director of the now-defunct Kenosha Institute of the Arts. "Do you know anyone in Kenosha who teaches hand drums?" I asked her.

"No," Kathy answered, do *you*?"

I suggested Tom to her and after a series of telephone conversations between them Tom agreed to come to Kenosha to teach a six-week course on hand drums that spring. Additionally, Kathy arranged for Tom to do an after-school program at the Boys and Girls Club and facilitate a multi-cultural drum event at Carthage College also in Kenosha.

Before any of these things took place, I discovered that drums were also making themselves heard with others in Kenosha. In late January, I was celebrating the Chinese New Year at a restaurant with a friend named Rosemary, who I hadn't seen in some time. As we caught up on our recent doings, she told me that on a recent trip to New Mexico she had visited a village where they made hand drums. She said she had been captivated by the sound of the Native American drum and was thinking about purchasing one.

Pausing, I exclaimed, "You'll never guess what I just got into—drumming!" I shared my New Year's Day adventures with her, and we exchanged ideas about this "drumming thing" that had come into both of our lives. Rosemary, a massage therapist, had read of the drum's use in ancient cultures as a tool for physical and emotional healing. I told her about my own "drum awakening" and informed her that a drum class would be offered at the Kenosha Institute of the Arts in April.

Rosemary and I both signed up for Kenosha's first hand drum class, which began on April 14, 2000. For something that had never been offered in our town before, it is worth noting that first drum class had six participants. The group was predominantly women ranging in age from 30-50. Of the two men, one was an elementary school teacher; the other a young man referred to the class as a form of therapy by his social worker.

In the next few weeks I worked hard to learn the material Tom presented. Drawing on the teaching traditions of several drum cultures, he told us, "If you can say it, you can play it." Following this mantra we learned how to play low and high tones on our drums using words or phrases such as, "Mama Pappa," "Mississippi Hot Dog" and "Hi, How-Are You?"

These were not ethnically specific rhythms of Africa, but a good way to get into using our drums. The pace picked up when we began venturing into West African rhythms including "Fanga" and "African Ibo." The most challenging drum rhythm for me was one part to a song called "Nigerian High Life." Tom introduced it towards the end of the six-week class and compared to what we had mastered so far, this was a rather complex rhythm. Where some of the songs had patterns of four or maybe eight beats, this one had one cycle of 16 beats—a lot to remember for beginners. I left the class thinking I would never get this rhythm.

It was now the end of May and one day I decided to take Millie outside to play music in the sunshine of our backyard. After warm-up exercises and all of the simple songs I knew, I took a run at "Nigerian High Life." I kept faltering; I'd get one cycle but was not able to start the next without pausing. Finally, I just kept my hands moving and the song emerged—all 16 notes of it. More importantly, I realized there was a song within a song—all of the low notes seemed linked together in something that resembled a pattern known as the "3-2 clave." The song "Nigerian High Life" was a high point in my drum studies so far.

It took a bit longer, however, to become at ease with other aspects of drumming. Even though I was able to conquer "Nigerian High Life," I began to realize that it was very difficult for me to "go off the menu" of well-learned patterns. Tom had demonstrated how subtle shifts in notes or timing could produce endless variations on simple themes, but more often than not I froze up as I attempted to improvise. For me it was the difference between swinging back and forth on a trapeze and actually letting go to catch the next swing—it was a leap of faith I was not yet ready to make.

Hand drumming turned out to be more involved than I first thought. Here I am seen listening carefully as I add something to the song at a lakefront drum circle in Milwaukee, mid-summer 2000.

I mentioned this concern to Tom, and he pointed out that the rhythms I knew well were very important to drum circles because they provided support to other drummers. Still, I wished I could feel comfortable leaving that steady ground to experiment and improvise and I often felt outclassed by more experienced or more natural drummers. What some might chalk up to "beginner's jitters" became a bugaboo for me. I felt I was musically defective if I couldn't shift a few notes in a familiar song and still play the song. From May through August 2000, I continued to play but felt stuck in a rut of my own making. By mid-August I almost despaired of playing the djembe in or out of a group.

During this time, Roger had also become quite attached to drumming. By May he had acquired his own djembe and had begun to enjoy the drum without lessons. Roger, it turned out, was a "drum natural" who could play rhythms by ear.

When Roger's work schedule changed, he decided to take formal drum lessons and I decided that the solution to my own drum quandary was more drum instruction. In mid-summer we found a drum class that would be held in Milwaukee starting in September. This class was to be led by McKinley Perkins, education director and choreographer of an African drum and dance troupe called Ko-Thi (pronounced Ko-thee).

Before we began our lessons with Mac I again shared drumming doubts with Tom. On Aug. 19, I received an interesting response. Tom didn't say, "There, there, you're a perfectly fine drummer, you just lack confidence." Instead he forwarded me information about a weekend retreat featuring several nationally known drum teachers, ethnic dancers and the "father of drum circle facilitation," Arthur Hull.

One of the weekend's presenters was to be female djembe artist and songwriter Ubaka Hill. One of the first professional recordings of djembe music that I had heard had been Ubaka's album *Shapeshifters*. Discovering that she would be teaching at this drumming retreat/conference sweetened the deal for my wanting to attend. In a departure from my usual family-first mindset, I delegated domestic obligations and rearranged my schedule at the newspaper so I could participate in this weekend at a retreat center in Linwood, Kansas. I was convinced that these instructors and these workshops were crucial to my spiritual growth. Additionally, I believed that between Friday and Sunday I would somehow be magically transformed into the djembe player I thought I wanted to be.

Magic and transformation did take place, but as so often happens, just not the way I thought they would.

Chapter 5

The Barry Experience

The rattle.
A tool...an instrument of
transition...from
one place or stage to another.

"Oya"—wind
of change
of cleansing
of whirling violent power

A whisper grows
and gives voice to our
living tornados.
—"Spiral Series I,"
10/9/00

In the brochure, the weekend in Linwood, Kansas, was simply titled "4th Annual Unity With A Beat! Weekend Retreat." For me it was more—it was change personified. In the first draft of this book I was planning to briefly describe this weekend. It was soon promoted to its own chapter because those two days were for me a watershed, not a footnote.

"Unity With A Beat!" at Tall Oaks Conference Center, Linwood, Kan., was one of a series of weekend retreats coordinated by Barry Bernstein, founder of Healthy Sounds, a consulting service focusing on rhythm and music in Overland Park, Kansas. For several years Barry had offered two-day retreats featuring some of the best talents in hand percussion, movement and healing music at a very affordable cost.

Friday night through early Sunday afternoon, Oct. 6-8, I found myself in the company of some 75 drum-minded folks from around the country. Some, like me, were very new to drumming; some very experienced; still others had had no previous exposure to drumming or drum culture whatsoever.

The weekend would include a djembe workshop with Ubaka Hill, drum circle facilitation training with Arthur Hull, frame drumming with Randy Crafton and "Imagery-based Drumming" with Louise DiMicelli-Mitran. Additionally, there would be a presentation of Native American dance and drumming, West African dance and a Sunday morning meditation led by Ubaka accompanied by Australian didjeridus, rattles and gongs.

Any one of these would have served as a very rich and rewarding musical experience. But there was all of this, all in one place. And there was more. Not listed on the schedule of events were the impromptu music jams that lasted until 3 a.m. These had the effect of creating a tribe within a tribe of people bonded by rhythm and, not insignificantly, sleeplessness.

The first of these late-night drum jams took place Friday night after an already full first day. Since early afternoon we had worked with Arthur on drum circle facilitation, participated in an after-dinner facilitated drum jam and watched a performance of Native American drum and dance. At 10 p.m., Barry requested we vacate the main hall out of consideration for workshop instructors whose sleeping quarters were nearby.

The request was noted but could not be followed. Many folks cleared out for walks in the woods or back to their respective bunkhouse quarters, but others lingered, talking quietly and showing one another instruments they had brought to play during the weekend. Since this *was* a group of worked-up musicians in a room full of percussion toys, it was not long before the inevitable happened. One musician demonstrated her silver flute to a percussionist who joined her on his didjeridu. They were soon accompanied by the lilting melody of mallets against the wooden keys of an African *balafone*, and the "jam that was not supposed to be" began.

Music interspersed with conversation continued until 3 a.m. Although we were gently asked more than once to consider making music elsewhere, 10 to 15 of us remained rooted to the room, unwilling to break the spell of our musical camaraderie. By 1 a.m. we were only four: two men and two women. Sitting knee to knee barely drumming, we spoke our stories, sharing a few stones from the paths that had led us to this place and this weekend.

Preparing this writing, I re-listened to cassette tapes I made during this weekend. Memory had served that this evening was one long magical moment in which I reveled. Re-hearing the first cassette of the weekend, however, I remembered that I personally entered that jam session in a very different frame of mind and spirit. I hear myself talking too much, laughing nervously and trying to play instruments that would fit into the beautiful songs that were emerging. I recall being quite unsure of myself—I felt unable to complement the drum rhythms that were going on and did not have any "cool" instruments like a balafone or didjeridu (nor any idea of how to play those, either). I hear myself playing some off-beat rhythms using a shaker and clave sticks. Wincing a bit, I know it is me I hear because I was closest to the tape recorder.

Yet the reason my memory had told me it was "all good" is because, ultimately, it all was. In the course of those five hours something shifted in me that helped me realize that *whatever* I contributed—that night and in the future—would be more than OK. Somewhere between the bits of forbidden music and discussions on under-the-ground houses and mind-altering mushrooms, I discovered self-acceptance and perhaps, absolution for my musical "sins."

Three retreat participants share a relaxed moment at breakfast on Saturday morning. From left, Anita Schnee, Tom Gill, Lorraine Achey.

By the next day my frame of mind was a crazy soup of peace and elation, light-heartedness and light-headedness (the last probably due to sleep deprivation). The next day—which was actually the same day, just a few hours later—Barry introduced the assembled workshop participants to the poetry of a 13th century Persian mystic writer named Jelaluddin

Rumi. A deep spiritual thinker who belonged to a community of spirit-minded folks (not unlike the retreat goers), Rumi, Barry told us, spent much time on the Sufi concept of *zikir*—which translates as "remembrance of the divine" within and around us. Rumi and his community explored this idea in poetry and ecstatic dance so powerful it translates from his time to ours.

Although I had not heard of Rumi before this, I was instantly in tune with his take on things. Barry sang one of Rumi's poems as he played the *doumbek* (a Middle Eastern drum), and I imagined Rumi's words addressing me, and my cohorts of the night before:

> When I am with you, we stay up all night.
> When you're not here, I can't go to sleep.
> Praise God for these two insomnias!
> And the difference between them.

Amusingly, and not surprisingly, at the time I was sure Barry had sung *insomniacs*, rather than *insomnias*.

As the weekend continued, we experienced rhythm in song, dance, meditation and drums. We held hands as we stood in concentric circles, we passed shaker eggs and breathed deeply. We envisioned our ancestors while the drones of didjerdus vibrated our bodies. We spent nights sharing stories and creating improvised music outdoors around the bonfire. By Sunday afternoon we had become a 75-member clan connected by the pulse of the drum and the simple joy of just being alive.

A panoramic view of the "Unity With A Beat!", tribe seen here on Sunday morning. Far left, seated on a chair, is Ubaka Hill. Sitting on floor in foreground is Barry Bernstein.

Photo by Tom Gill

I had attended that weekend hoping for a blast of drum instruction that would put me over the hump to becoming a "real" drummer. I also thought

I should see how Arthur Hull taught people in case I wanted to lead drum circles some day. Did I come away from the weekend a great drummer? Was I ready to facilitate large groups of people at a single bound? Not really. But something did happen. What seemed like monumental change was, in hindsight, just a new phase of the change that had begun on January 1, by the lakefront in Milwaukee.

The past 10 months had opened doors to different types of drummers and drumming. I had taken classes with Tom and had begun technically demanding sessions with the African drummers of Milwaukee. During the weekend at Barry's, I had studied with Ubaka. The journey so far had been both exhilarating and frustrating.

What became clear during "Unity With A Beat!" was that rhythm could actually create community and bonds between strangers that transcended all outward differences of age, race or ability. This effectively translated into a personal vision: I now knew the mission for me was less about becoming a skilled djembe player than it was about finding a way to invite others to share this amazing experience.

During the weekend Ubaka had led us through rhythm parts to a song she had written called "Oya's Song." Ubaka explained that Oya is the African god, or *orisha*, of the wind. She said her song refers to Oya as the "wind of change," both literally and symbolically. She told us "Oya" is pronounced "Oh, yah." For me, nothing could have been closer to the truth.

As we said our goodbyes around the large circle in the main room, Barry and Arthur invited each of us to declare some kind of intention for whatever we might want to do after the weekend was over. When it was my turn, I told fellow retreat-goers that I would go back to my small town and "grow community" through drumming.

Chapter 6

Opening our Doors:
Rhythm in the Round

> People are looking for a place where their
> individuality will be honored, where their
> personal gifts can be freely made available
> to serve the greater good.
>
> —Malidoma Patrice Somé,
> *The Healing Wisdom of Africa*

As I left the "Unity With A Beat!" Retreat, I was on a rhythmic high that nearly made the United flight redundant. Before the engines were even to full throttle I did what I always do when faced with a new and exciting phase in my life—I began to write.

Between Oct. 8, 2000, and Nov. 27, 2002, I filled six spiral-bound notebooks with insights, revelations, dreams and crushing disappointments. Even before I scribbled my first thoughts I sensed these notebooks would become tributaries of the same stream—a stream flowing to some deep pool. With this in mind I decided to create a series of notebooks designated by roman numerals.

Titling the books "Spiral Series" was a play on words—referring to the physical entity of the type of notebook and also a newly obtained perspective on the word "spiral." During his the weekend Barry and other retreat leaders had used the "spiral" in word and image as a metaphor for interconnectedness—an image of circles connected one to the next, and a spiral-shaped journey that leads us home to our spiritual selves.

I started the series in a red-covered spiral-bound notebook, cousin to the one in which I began this work. The first thoughts on the first pages were, in retrospect, fairly incoherent. They reflect a state of mind that, although electrically charged, was also thoroughly unfocused. After the title page and pages to which I taped my travel itinerary and "Unity With A Beat!" brochure, the writings went like this:

Workshop Notes 10/8/00

At the airport
make tape copies for Lorraine —
Ubaka Hill
Michaelene—late nite jam #1
Call/email (arrow) Nancy F.'s
phone/e-mail
Susan
All tapes for Lorraine except
Frame Drum w/ Barry
mid East OK

On the next pages semi-complete sentences emerge:

Speaking of hallucinations I thought
the orange safety lights on landing
tarmac equipment were a whole
bunch of pumpkins.

"Live Wire" poem
Buzzed on being
but being beyond self.

Hearing new notes.
Humming of human voices
Airplane machinery or awareness?

The "doum" of the frame drum.
Douming along somewhere under
me...to the right underside of this
vehicle.

As we lift into the air the tune
becomes "Mahnjani"
I'm getting the bell part now
Under the whir of "bum-
bumbumbum"
Over and again, bells 4/5?

In keeping with a personal journaling style, the words and ideas ebb and flow between expression of organized thought and the random jottings of an overheated mind. Phrases that reoccurred with some frequency were "emergence" and "change at a cellular level."

I go on at length about the "Spiral Series" because it served as a link, connecting that first retreat weekend to my commitment to community drumming. I eventually "came down" enough to function in my family and at my day job, but the energy I felt at that time served as fuel to stoke fires for community drumming in Kenosha.

Coming home I knew that the first manifestation of "growing community" for drummers in Kenosha would be home-based drum circles. Even before the retreat weekend, Roger and I had begun to explore the possibility of hosting circles at our house. The idea, in late spring 2000, was for me to practice what I learned in Tom's class by inviting fellow drum students to the house. Roger and I figured it would be sort of like drum circles we had experienced elsewhere—except in Kenosha at that time we only knew of about four people who played hand drums!

Before we opened up our home, we had to take into consideration that we had young children who might not appreciate sharing their home with strangers and loud percussive sounds. We looked to Tom Gill's circles as a model. Tom had managed to create a space in the basement of his house in which friends and strangers played percussion-based music for three hours at a time twice a month.

Even with this example, the decision to open our house to drum circles was not an easy one. Our children were seven and 11 at the time and neither Alex nor Lauren had shown much interest in or tolerance for the drums. We were asking them to share their home with complete strangers who would be making this not-so-desirable music for several hours on end. After a few family meetings it was decided circles could take place with the condition that the music be limited to three hours and cease by 9 p.m.

We chose to offer the space of our fairly large living room to hold circles on the second Saturday of every month. We selected that time slot because weekdays were filled with the family business of homework. We also didn't want to compete with ongoing Thursday circles in Milwaukee. Additionally, the wordsmith in me rather liked the alliteration: "Second Saturdays on Seventh Avenue at Six."

Our intention was to offer a place for hand drummers, but also others who were musically inclined. In short, we wanted to be all-inclusive and believed that all creative comers should be welcome. Thinking about a name for this venture, we considered something that said, "We are something new in Kenosha." One early idea was "Alternative Musicians of Kenosha" whose acronym would read "A.M.O.K." as in "running amok" but this, we felt, was too "out there" even by our standards.

It wasn't long before we hit on a winner—"Rhythm in the Round." From what we had seen so far the success of drum events was based on people sitting together in a circle—none leading, but all sharing and learning from one another. We soon created a logo to carry the theme: words written in a circle around a stylized drawing of a djembe, our first drum.

Our logo, designed by us and cleaned up and reworked on computer by Tom Gill, who also operates a graphic design business.

Soon after deciding to share our home with fellow drummers, we realized this great idea might take a little time to catch on in our area. Located 55 miles north of Chicago and 45 miles south of Milwaukee, on the map Kenosha looks like it might be a crossroads for hip sub-urban culture. However, it appeared that said modern culture had taken a detour around Kenosha County. From the time we arrived from Chicago in 1989 until the time we thought about holding drum circles in 2000, we had observed an entrenched cultural conservatism. Although many people had moved to Kenosha from Chicago and Milwaukee during this time, efforts to introduce new things—dark roast coffee in restaurants or anything but Danielle Steele-oriented bookstores—had been quashed by lack of community support.

Despite or perhaps in spite of this, Roger and I set our sights on holding a space for drummers in our living room. We could have opted to drive to Milwaukee and Chicago for our drum circle fix. But something told us there might just be other "closet creatives" in Kenosha looking for a place to express themselves, and we believed we should be the ones offering that place.

Our first home circles were lightly attended, to say the least. We opened our doors to drumming in May but it was a while before there were more than three of us making music in the living room on any given second Saturday.

August was the turning point for Rhythm in the Round. Drumming found its way onto the cultural map of Kenosha thanks to local artists who hosted our monthly drum circle at their home. Sometime during the spring I was talking with an artist friend named Monne Haug about my discovery and enjoyment of drum circles when she suggested we hold a circle at her home, which offered a wilderness-like setting.

I was not sure we would have much of a crowd but took Monne up on her offer and set the date for the second Saturday in August. Roger and I sent word to the few drummers we knew in Kenosha and extended the invite to drum friends in Milwaukee. Somewhere along the way, this circle took on a life of its own and by noon on the second Saturday of August, 2000, our phone was ringing nonstop with people we had never met asking for directions to Monne and Fred's house. We later discovered our Kenosha friends knew other friends and our Milwaukee drum pals had told other drum pals. Additionally, Monne and Fred had invited family, neighbors and other artists to see what this drumming thing was all about.

The night drumming came to Kenosha: Artists and drummers play together at Monne and Fred's house on Aug. 12, 2000. Seen here from left, Gerhardt Kroll, Monne Haug and the author.

The August circle was indeed an event. What had been billed as a three-hour circle lasted long into the evening with drumming and dancing on the patio and a stream of sparkling conversation held by the buffet table in Monne's house. That evening exposed people in Kenosha, who had never experienced in-the-moment music making, to community drumming at its best. Images from that evening include a short woman wildly shaking a rainstick to the beat of her own ecstatic dancing; a group of people playing Australian didjeridus and a conga line of artists winding their way through the trees playing shakers made from plumbing supplies.

The circle at Monne's also introduced Roger and me to the cultural side of Kenosha we had suspected was there all along. That night we connected with Melanie Hovey and Jamie Cassar, founders of a brand-new artists' cooperative called Lemon Street Gallery. We met people who would later come to our living room to play drums and other people who would teach our family members how to make books, create stained glass artwork and do watercolor painting.

On the second Saturday of the next month, people began to fill our living room space and continued to do so for the next few years. Amazingly, it was not the same collection of folks who had attended the circle at Monne's but some who were there and others who heard about it from people who had been there.

As our circle grew so did awareness of others on similar music-oriented paths. We discovered that earlier in the year a drum circle had begun in Racine, another mid-size town about 10 miles north of Kenosha. Tom Anger and Mercedes Dzindzeleta hosted a monthly drum circle on the Friday following the full moon at their storefront enterprise called Circles~Weave The Nurturing Center. In November, Roger and I attended that circle playing our djembes along with the frame drums and percussion toys shared by all. At Tom and Mercedes's circle we met people who would find their way down to Kenosha for our drum circles and many of our future drum-related events.

In December 2000, just two months after my retreat weekend, our drum circle reached critical mass—we "maxed out" our living room. Using every chair in our house, the 22-person circle featured artists from the circle at Monne's, several folks from the Racine circle and members of a local alternative rock band called the Boatbuilders. The incredible sound created by this diverse crowd was so musical and so big that I picked up the phone for Tom to have a listen—just in case he couldn't hear us in Milwaukee!

Like lyrics to a folk song: "Watch our circle grow"! Our December 2000 circle drew quite a crowd.

In the ensuing months, circle attendance continued to grow. Sometimes we had a tape recorder running, an attempt to hold onto musical moments that would otherwise be lost to mortal ears. We offered a table of snack foods and a notebook into which people could sign their names, addresses and e-mail addresses. Capturing names, we realized, was the single best way to continue the connection of these people to our circle and us to them. The list would also come in handy for a future electronic community newsletter.

During breaks between songs, artists, teachers, tax accountants and massage therapists shared stories and insights. By March, 2001, I began to speculate on this phenomena in my rapidly developing "Spiral Series." (Incredibly, only five months since Barry's retreat, I was working on Spiral IV.) I had decided our circles were something like the intellectual salons of early 20th century Paris.

> College girls drop by for a 'pre-party warm-up' and a Native American named Brandon reveals the mysteries of the sweat lodge. Somewhere in between two friends reconnect, bringing an unexpected gift and another new friend arrives with her soul burdened with concern for another friend. Did I leave anyone out? Not likely, for all are welcome...
>
> —"Spiral Series IV,"
> 3/10/00

Looking back, this time was a lot like "Love is the Only Power" a traditional folk song on Barry Bernstein's compact disk, *Songs of the Spirit:*

> Love is the only power,
> Love is the only way
> Love, Love, Love, Love
> Watch our circle grow.

I had pledged to grow a drum community in Kenosha—now the drum community had a life of its own. With virtually no external advertising, new people were finding their way to us to check out the circle and create impromptu music.

One Wednesday night about eight of us were practicing some African drum rhythms in our living room when the doorbell rang. Assuming it was another player arriving later than usual, I opened the door but discovered a man who I did not recognize.

"Is someone playing drums here?" this stranger asked.

"Yes," I said, "Are you with the police and is someone complaining about the noise?"

"No," said the man, "My name is Ed, I'm from around the corner and I've been playing drums all my life. I happened to be passing and I heard drumming so thought I'd check it out."

With that, Ed was ushered in and invited to sit down and play with us. He told us his family was from Puerto Rico and he had been raised around drumming and rhythm. He had been in several bands and was glad to find drummers in the area to play with.

In the spring of 2003 we discovered the extensive vibrations from our monthly musical adventures had begun to take a toll on our 74-year-old home. When Roger found wood floor shims had been shaken from the basement rafters, we realized it was time to move our "rhythmic family reunions" to the basement. Over the course of that summer we took back 260-square feet of our home, reclaiming walls previously covered in mildew, relocating or tossing old furniture and evicting the resident spiders.

From living room to basement space, many people have walked through our doors for many diverse reasons and in many different ways. They come to play instruments and they come with their stories. We have learned that these life stories and tales are vital to the life of the circle. If some days we talk more than we play, we know that holding a space for the nurturing of spirit is at least as important as are drum and bell parts of a song.

Stories from people who have come to play music with us indicate that the drum circle fills an important need. Maybe it is gratitude for being accepted into the circle unconditionally. Maybe it is simply the need to be needed. In the words of Malidoma Patrice Somé:

> In indigenous cultures, people relate to
> one another in terms of what each brings

to the village, not in terms of how one appears.

Our part has been to build the village and hold the space where people, especially adults, can feel safe as they explore the creative side of their nature. In return we become recipients for the joy and delight felt by those who have joined us. One story that best sums this up is that of Kathy Carson, a special education teacher in Racine. She came to our house after meeting us at Tom and Mercedes' circle.

"As I child I always wanted to play the drums," Kathy said. "I was told that girls didn't play drums so my parents made me play the clarinet. I am so glad I met you guys—now I can follow my bliss."

We know it's not us or anything special we did. Kathy brought her own bliss to the circle—we just opened the door.

Chapter 7

Stepping into the Circle

*I fear public speaking—to an
extreme degree. I do not believe
then, that God wants me to live my
calling by addressing crowds in
public.*

—Author journal,
3/15/98

Tuesday April 10, 2001: I am standing in a darkened convention hall in downtown Milwaukee. I am one of ten musicians, poised with drums, bells and tambourines. In the center of the room a spotlight pops on, illuminating a beautiful African woman in a glistening white gown. She calls out into the cavernous darkness. We respond in rhythm on our instruments. The house lights begin to glow and we start to play, entering the dining area filled with 1,500 luncheon-goers. Strangely, I am not afraid.

On a Sunday morning in September 2004, I am standing in front of 300 people at a church service. I am not part of a cortege of drum pals and I am 250 miles from home. I have just conducted a drum circle for 60 adults and children and am now about to address the congregation. Stepping up to the microphone I see the sea of faces and two things hit me simultaneously: 1) I am terrified beyond belief; 2) these people need to hear the story of the song "Fanga"—an African song of peace and welcome—and I am the one who has to tell it.

The story is told, drumming begins and several of the 300 churchgoers begin to sing and play parts to "Fanga," a song first introduced to this country by the late Nigerian drummer and teacher Babatunde Olatunji.

From 1998 to 2004, I had come a long, long way. "How" this came to be is really the story of "why" and the subject of this particular chapter.

As a child, a teen and for most of my adult life, I have suffered from public-induced nervousness that has ranged from blushing when called on to read in class to shaking my wedding bouquet into a shower of soggy petals. Addressing groups of people—defined by me as "more than two"—has often resulted in a dry mouth, blurred vision and rapid heartbeat—symptoms common to your basic irrational-type phobia.

It may just be that I am "wired" for shyness. An early contributing factor were frequent relocations made by my family due to my father's employment with Amoco Oil Company. Moving several times—from New York to Illinois (twice), over to England and back to Illinois—my siblings and I were always "the new kids on the block." Making friends was risky business so, choosing the road less traveled, I became a reader, a diary writer and a bit of an introvert.

My career choice, journalism, was based on the intention to become more outgoing. As a teen I saw myself becoming a solitary novelist, but as a young adult I selected a vocation in which a good news story depended on the ability to speak to people, gain their trust and elicit interesting details of their lives.

Somewhere during the next 20 years as a magazine and newspaper reporter I discovered that I really liked people. I particularly enjoyed telling the stories of people who would otherwise not be heard. I was able to express myself and still remain in the background.

Reflecting on my role as a writer, in 1999 I wrote the following in a journal:

> I become a pass-through for others, a mediator, translator, messenger; a catalyst and a connector...I am called to paint the picture but not be in it myself.

By the time I wrote this reflection a chain of events was already in motion that would create a shift in this perception. That was the time of reading books that urged me to assess where I was and where I might want to go in life. When the new direction revealed itself—when drums came into my life and the lives of my family—it was no longer possible to stand on the sidelines and write the stories of other people's lives. It was time to step into my own circle.

Stepping into the circle happened both suddenly and subtly. It seemed like the most natural thing in the world to do and at the same time took a monumental leap of faith.

My call to serve community drum circles began nearly as soon as Roger and I opened the doors for our home circles. During breaks between drum songs people would say things like "Wow, this is so much fun, have you ever taken the drums to schools?" Or, "My co-workers would love this. Maybe you could do a program for us sometime."

At first the answer was, "I don't do this but I know someone in Milwaukee who does," and would promptly produce one of Tom Gill's business cards.

Pretty soon, despite a fear of public speaking, my passion for drumming made me want to say "yes." The more I witnessed excitement created by group drumming at our house, the more I realized that it was something that needed to be shared outside the house as well. It was time to expand on my personal pledge "to grow community."

One of the things that helped me overcome initial fears was that for most of my life sharing has come pretty easily to me. In college I lived in a church-run co-op where community living was the order of the day. After initial shyness (of course) I became quite comfortable sharing space and household duties with my peers.

When people asked me if I would share drumming with others, I thought, "Sure, since I'm the one with the cool drum toys I should be sharing them." I soon discovered, however, that it is one thing to decide to share the fun of drumming with others and another thing to actually do it. I began to learn—from Tom, Arthur and personal experience—that "sharing my percussion toys" is something called a "facilitated drum circle." In other words, to share drums successfully I had to face my public speaking demons—and win.

So what *is* this drum circle facilitation and why is it such a big deal? A facilitated drum circle takes place when someone with percussion instruments—goatskin headed, wood-bodied djembes; plastic buckets with oak dowel mallets; pot lids, etc.—takes said instruments to a gathering (2-2,000 people give or take) and shapes an interlude of interactive music. This generally involves inviting people to experiment with the instruments, and then gently molding the group's musical efforts through the use of universal body language.

In other words: the facilitator is the complete focus of attention of a possibly large group of strangers. They may or may not even want to play the drums but depend on the facilitator to tell them what to do for the next hour (or until they feel comfortable making music on their own). The prospects were—and can still be—terrifying.

My first exposure to a facilitated drum event was on April 12, 2000. Tom Gill had been invited by the Kenosha Institute of the Arts to lead an event at Carthage College in Kenosha titled, "Music, Language and Literature Extravaganza with Diversity Drumming." I had been acquainted with my drum for only a few months but Tom asked me to come to the stage area and assist him. My job was to simply strike a barrel-shaped drum with a stick at an even tempo for about five minutes, but the thought that kept running through my mind was, "Oh God, look at all those people staring up here."

For two hours after that, Tom animatedly addressed the group, shaping music created by school-age children, college students and adults using a combination of spoken metaphors and body language. Back in my seat I was impressed and entertained by the show but I could not imagine myself doing that.

Yet, something had grabbed my curiosity, and over the next few months I found myself attending drum circles facilitated by Tom and others in Milwaukee and Chicago. Watching the person in the center of the circle, I marveled at the strange, wonderful and slightly weird chemistry that took place between that person and all kinds of people, from at-risk-youth to Alzheimer's sufferers. A room full of strangers who had never seen one another before and a mix of rhythm instruments looked like a recipe for unmitigated chaos of the noisy variety. But—it wasn't. Within 15 minutes of the first drumbeat, people began playing together, having fun and sounding like a band that had been practicing a musical piece for weeks.

As that first year of drumming and watching circles progressed, I began to consider the possibility of trying this facilitation thing myself. It still looked difficult and still involved being in front of an audience, but this was *drums* after all, and drums are fun and good for people and...

...And so, after Tom finished a series of drum circles in Kenosha at the Boys and Girls Club, it was suggested that I continue the program. Me, who owned maybe three "real" drums and some shakers filled with popcorn, I should step into a gym with 20 kids wound up after a whole day of school and help them make music...So I said, "yes."

My first solo moments in the center of the circle were not pretty. The logistics, as described above, were intimidating from the start. When Tom was at the Boys and Girls Club, the kids had been noisy and active, but he managed eventually to get them together on the same musical page. When I showed up it was a different story. Maybe it was my equipment—a sorry assortment of so-called instruments compared to Tom's collection of nice African drums—or maybe it was that these guys instinctively knew I was terrified of them. It was probably a little of both.

I started out bravely. Remembering things I'd seen Tom do, I would hand out my few instruments, try to ignore cries of "I don't want to play *this*, I want *that one!*" and encourage the kids to play the four-beat rhythm "Mama Pappa." But even when some cooperated, they were soon completely bored by the "1-2-3-4" rhythm and would revert to banging randomly on anything in the room, and occasionally each other.

Boredom, I began to see, was in fact *the* problem. What I needed was a way to keep the music going and the kids engaged and excited about playing it. I did not yet have any neat tricks—my only training had been observing Tom, but at those events I was usually in the circle as a participant and not taking notes. Additionally, I was also trying to stave off possible panic attacks from: 1) being in front (or in the middle of) a group of people and 2) not knowing what I was doing in front of this group of people.

During the summer and fall of 2000, I continued to muddle through sessions at the Boys and Girls Club, but, as I said, it was challenging. Because facilitation was not my strong point, I sought other ways to reach these children. During a few sessions we made rainsticks from large cardboard tubes filled with pebbles. I also used the time to teach the beginner rhythms I knew. One week I learned a three-part song from a student who had heard it in music class at school. I called the rhythms "Vincent's Song" after the student who taught it to me. I later discovered that the parts were from a song created by Will Schmidt, a Milwaukee music teacher, but to me it will always be "Vincent's Song."

Despite success with these students I was still frustrated by my lack of facilitation skill. For advice I turned to *Drum Circle Spirit*, written by the "father of drum circle facilitation," Arthur Hull. He offered all kinds of really cool techniques for drum circle management, but hadn't exactly covered what to do if you have crappy instruments, wild kids and are by nature a rather shy person. Those lessons, I realized, were my own to learn.

The wonder of it is that something *did* drive me to learn these lessons.

I had a fine day job—the *Kenosha News* was paying me well to write interesting articles—I didn't need to learn how to do something that was frustrating and complicated and never the same twice...or did I?

Apparently, I did. Something was driving me to explore this unknown territory called rhythm facilitation—to seek knowledge and experience so that I could get better at something I already loved.

Priceless knowledge and experience sometimes find their way to our door when we least expect them. Long before I entertained the idea of facilitating circles I had a conversation with a news source that had significant implications for my future drum path. Sometime in spring of 2000, I was working on a feature story on the topic of the "importance of play." One of my sources was Rita Klinkhammer, then in charge of a toy-lending library in Racine. She talked about how play enriches the lives of children and adults and I shared my newly acquired fascination with playing hand drums. She said she had no experience with drum circles but was intrigued. We then discussed how drumming might be useful for preschool-age children and caregivers. I told her that Tom might be someone who could tell her more and/or provide her with a drum circle experience.

Sometime between April 12, 2000 and Jan. 29, 2001, Rita met Tom. Tom facilitated drum circles for the Toy Lending Library, and Rita decided *I* should conduct a series of drum circles for preschools in spring 2001. During a small circle on Jan. 29, 2001, Tom introduced me as an "official co-facilitator" to a room of 15 preschool teachers and launched me into the circle.

Tom's declaring me a "real live drum facilitator" was a leap of faith for all parties concerned. Until that point my drum circle facilitation had consisted of the Boys and Girls Club experiments and a few workshop exercises with Arthur Hull. Now I was in the middle of a small circle of respectful adults patiently waiting for my instructions. For me, this was even more intimidating than a roomful of wild kids. But there was something, maybe magic, that helped me accept the challenge. These women were interested—as interested as I had been when I first saw a drum—and they wanted to play. Tom had gotten them going and had me step in for a while. I don't recall what I did—maybe I just had some of the women stop playing while others listened, and I am sure it was very, very brief—but we all survived the experience. I was nervous but made the attempt because

I knew I needed to learn how to offer this cool thing to people who might find it as fun as I did.

Then a curious thing happened. Sometime between Jan. 29 and March 4 I got scared. Very scared. I experienced a crisis of confidence that nearly derailed my drum path for good.

This crisis was triggered on March 2 after a seemingly innocent drum circle in a coffee shop in Hartford, Wisconsin. I had accompanied Tom to the drum circle he was facilitating in hopes of picking up more circle-leading techniques. In the middle of a rather groovy song played by energetic 20-year-olds, Tom suggested I do "something." Frozen with fear but aware this was what I said I wanted, I stepped into the circle taking the cowbell and stick offered to me. The only thing I could think to do was to stop the song and shift it to something else. The music stopped all right—then everyone got up and left to get another round of café latte.

The next day I kicked myself for having "crashed the circle." I turned to my journal for solace:

> Doubt finds openings created
> by sleeplessness, lack of proper
> nutrition and over-stimulation from
> all quarters. Today I had hoped
> I could clear the decks of doubt
> but find I'm way too tired to clean
> anything up—too much work…
> easier to say—I can't.
>
> Can't what? Face the possibility
> that I am not called to be a drum
> circle facilitator or even master my
> own rhythms? That my calling may
> in fact put me on the side or even
> outside the circle?
>
> Today I wanted to wake up fresh.
> Ready to say, "yes" again. The
> best I can say is "I don't know."
> Maybe that's OK, too. I am going

> to be the support rhythm and be
> happy with it...

> —"Spiral Series IV,"
> 3/3/01

In this same journal entry, I ponder whether I should pursue facilitation by working harder at it or running away from it altogether. I also recognize that sometimes I just get too tired to see the forest for the trees. In the end I set a timetable to achieve certain goals.

> If, for example, I am still stuck
> six months from now, there's a
> problem...OK, Aug. 1, 2001.
> Maybe five months is enough.
> Enough to know what's possible.
> Enough time to accept the not-
> possible. The point at which I
> say I'm ready to sell something
> good (to schools which start in
> September) or admit I don't have
> anything to offer—not so much
> nothing but not the lessons or
> facilitation (maybe I will run the
> Kenosha Institute of the Arts
> coffee shop and book the talents of
> other performers...)

Deadline assigned, it was time to put aside my fear and honor the commitments at hand. I knew I had little time to worry about my facilitation skills—or even if I had enough musical instruments—because Rita had already promoted me to several preschools in Kenosha. She had arranged for me to introduce instruments to children (age 1 to 5) and their teachers at four daycare facilities (two times each) in the next three weeks.

My personal calendar went into overtime: one day I might start at the *News*, write for an hour, jump into my car, manage the chaos of 40 young children banging on oatmeal boxes, then go back to the *News* and write for three more hours. Sandwiched around this were the schedules and needs of my own kids—Alex, then age eight, and Lauren, then 12. It was also

March in Wisconsin and several of these drum circles took place on days when it was raining, snowing and sometimes a fun mixture of both.

As for the facilitating, there were good moments, just plain noise and many lessons clearly not found in any "Facilitators' Handbook"! Sometimes I'd arrive at the basement of a church that had lots of stairs and long hallways, or a room with no space, or too many babies crying for naps. Often it was just kids banging on things and grabbing each other's instruments. But sometimes we would all be banging, shaking and clacking on the same rhythm. And sometimes kids would sing or dance a little dance, and it was a good day.

On the good days I discovered that I learned while they learned. From these first forays into the circle I learned the most critical of all facilitation lessons: "Adapt, adapt, adapt!" I quickly found with this age group a "lesson plan" was more a "serving suggestion." I may have come in with the intention of presenting "Mama Pappa" but if a three-year-old began a chorus of "Twinkle, Twinkle Little Star" that's where things went for a while.

The bottom line—or top, since it's a circle you never know—is that if I, as a facilitator, say I provide "interactive music" then, by definition, the event no longer belongs to me. The circle belongs to and is shaped by whoever is in it, no matter what age.

On days when there was less magic than mayhem, when I questioned what I was doing, or why, Rita dropped by with an abundance of encouragement. She'd tell me that the preschool teachers thought it was wonderful, that the kids had had fun and that I seemed to be "as flexible as Gumby" (a rubbery toy from the 1960s).

Rita's feedback served as a source of inspiration and energy because I found myself saying "yes" to new adventures even while I was learning from those first preschool circles.

> In the span of one week I said
> "yes" to a school of grades 1-5 in
> Brookfield, a gathering of nuns
> and monks in Racine and a camp
> of children afflicted with muscular
> dystrophy in Salem (Wisconsin)....
> no time for fear or doubt or even
> "what if": onward and into the fray.

—"Spiral Series IV,"
March 19, 2001

As I said "yes" to these events, I kept trying new things for new groups: buying a few more drums and making instruments from oak dowels, plastic toilet parts and 5-gallon olive containers (minus the Greek olives). We loaded our drums onto a golf cart and drove through a campground in the rain; found ourselves in a room full of chairs with desktops (a big problem when you have a big drum on the floor in front of you); and lugged armloads of drums up and down stairs. There were times when people didn't get why they were there or really didn't care and other times when kids smacked things so hard that instruments broke.

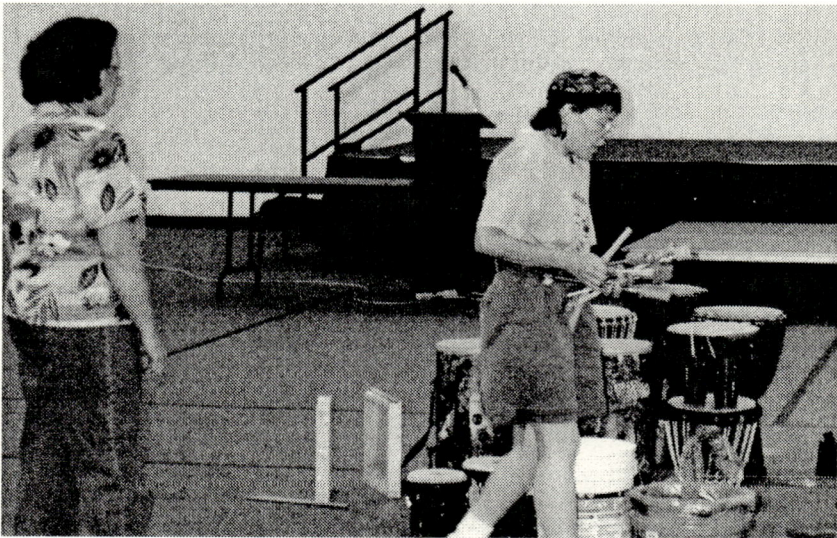

**"Let's see, that's ten mallets, 15 drums and 120 kids and adults."
The author, right, counts mallets for participants of her first large
drum circle, a camp for children with muscular dystrophy. At left,
Rosemary Worth, a friend who volunteered to help, looks on.**

Even so, from the spring of 2001 I discovered that every drum circle was a learning opportunity—for those I came for and especially, myself. I learned that the only teaching is in the learning—even when I might think I understood the needs of a particular group, I was dealing with people and people have moods, attitudes and energies that change from day to day. I learned that my own nervousness and fear was secondary to the opportunity to share something I knew was fun and sometimes even good for your health.

Talking over successes and less-than-uplifting events with Tom, I discovered my experiences are similar to his and those of other rhythm facilitators. We realize that the intrinsic good of drumming is sometimes offset by the newness of this type of music. We agree that, more often than not, it's not "us"—or our talent as musicians—but the expectations or preconceptions of those in the circle.

One of the things that kept me going is also one of the most challenging aspects of rhythm facilitation—the format, the physical entity, of the circle. Asking people to interact, face-to-face in a circle is something new and a bit radical. This "something new" can be scary to some people. We live in a world where we are spoon-fed information and much of our recreation is enjoyed passively. The chance to engage with others is extremely rare. For some—particularly those who consider themselves "serious grown-ups"— non-scripted, spontaneous participation may seem threatening. If it exceeds their comfort zone their first reaction may be skeptical smirks and nervous chuckles. It is from this group that I have learned one of my biggest lessons: My job as a facilitator is less about directing music than it is about setting an atmosphere of security and trust where everyone is welcome to relax and just play. In this way skeptical smirks melt into grins of enjoyment.

Drum circle facilitation is a lot more than just showing up with drums. The author steps into the (big) circle, assisted on *djun djuns* **by husband, Roger.**

But for a vast majority—especially those with mental and physical challenges—a drum circle is refreshing opportunity for self-expression. How many times is a person with dementia asked for his or her opinion or creative input? How often can a man in a wheelchair with gnarled fingers and inch-thick glasses have 20 people cheer for him when he hits a drum with a mallet?

Because of all of this—the frustrations and the happy surprises—the experiment I tried for "five or six months" is now entering its sixth year. I knew had passed the point of no return when I was no longer asking, "Can I really get into the center of the circle and do this?" but was wondering, "Do I have enough instruments?" and "How many more can I make by next Saturday?"

Do I still get stage fright? Yes, every time, just before the first group song. But as I count up my equipment—enough to facilitate 130 at the time of writing—I think of the men, women and, yes, little crying babies who might be playing my pot lids and popcorn-filled shakers, and know I can and must step into the circle again.

Stage fright be gone! Here, the joy of sharing drums with students at Lincoln Middle School, Kenosha, overcomes the author's natural tendency towards shyness.

Arthur Hull says that rhythm facilitators tend to say "yes" first and worry about the details of the drum circle later. I felt the need to follow the way of the facilitator, but my first steps were guided by self-conscious fears. As it turned out, love overcame fear. Love of the circle, love of the good things that can happen in the circle, overcame the fear that was driven by worrying about myself. Stepping into the circle I essentially stepped into who I was meant to be.

> We don't choose callings—we answer them. We hear them when we are ready (our heart has special "ears"—tuning in when the time is right). People call—suggest something—when I answer "yes" then suddenly (so it seems) there's this new direction, calling...I could not have chosen it—it had to choose me, first.

I don't know I'm ready until I answer the call. To teach—to lead—to evangelize—my passion. The energy is already there, but the particular direction...comes from outside myself.

—"Spiral Series I,"
11/1/00

Chapter 8

Teachers, Mentors & Spirit Guides

In the past seven chapters I mentioned several of those to whom I owe this journey. Some of these are Tom Gill, Arthur Hull, Ubaka Hill, Barry Bernstein, Judy Piazza, Phil Jones, Malidoma Patrice Somé and Mickey Hart.

They are the obvious teachers. It is relatively easy—and imperative—to give thanks to those who have given us instruction and imparted their hard-earned wisdom. It is more complex, but just as necessary, to pay homage to those from whom we have learned vital-but-more-subtle-life lessons.

Among the many to be added to the "big names" list: Roger, the Wilson kids, singer/songwriter Jewel; our dog the late Emmit the retired racing greyhound; and Communication Workers of America, Local No. 34159.

I have chosen to acknowledge these teachers in a narrative format because: 1) I want to make this work optimally readable and, 2) Teachers are more than just a name, they are a story. Their stories are mine, woven into a tapestry of colors and textures. Pretty as may sound, the truth is that not all teachers lead by positive example—some are the grains of sand aggravating the oyster until it creates a pearl out of self defense.

In this litany of thanks I choose to begin with angels, saving the devils for later. Absolutely first on the list is Roger. Had he not picked up my drum Millie and played along with Santana music on the radio, I would never have engaged at this level. I could not in good faith have invested our family's financial resources in drums or have abandoned the home front to explore a passion that was mine alone. For me, it has always been a group thing, a tribal thing.

Next, there's our family dog, a retired racing greyhound named Emmit. We adopted him in May 1997, from the dog track in Kenosha. His markings appealed to our native motif—he was a black-striped orange-tinged brindle; the effect somewhere between zebra and tiger. He chose us and lived with us for seven years before he passed away at age 12 in October 2004.

Walking with Emmit or watching him run full tilt in the fenced-in ballpark, I was impressed by the dance of form and function within this creature. Like others of his breed, he was long-legged and streamlined—built for speed with no extra baggage. He walked in serene elegance but it was obvious he was ready to run at a moment's notice; the energy of his muscles nearly visible.

Poyners pre-drumming, pose for their 1997 Christmas card. From left, the author, Lauren, age 9 and Roger. In foreground, a patient Emmit sports reindeer antlers in the spirit of the season, hugged by Alex, age 5.

What was the lesson learned from Emmit and where does it connect to my drum path? In this animal I recognized—or perhaps remembered—the importance of honoring my own physical and spiritual energy. The callings and challenges I was beginning to explore were manifestations of something, like Emmit's nature, I was "wired for" from birth. I began to realize I had to do something to honor this predestined energy, even if it ran a very different race than the one I was currently in.

That race was the ratrace that had become my professional life at the *Kenosha News*. It was not so much the work—I had free reign with word crafting and a weekly food column with my picture at the top—it was the condition in which the work was produced. Like other newsroom employees, I was required to participate in the labor union, referred to as the "Guild." Throughout history labor unions have served a useful purpose. However, this particular union, at this point in time, had failed to address the needs of the many *Kenosha News* part-timers.

By 2002 I was working 30 hours per week—on paper, a part-timer. According to the contract part-timers were not granted paid sick time. In the ten-plus years I had worked at the *News*, the sick pay issue had been discussed but not rectified. When the three-year contract came up for re-negotiation in 2002 it was expected that, as usual, all members support the demands the union made on management. I decided "Not me, not this time." Drums and rhythm had helped me find my own peace and I found I was now out of rhythm with my workplace and co-workers.

Contract negotiations between union leaders and management began to look like hostage negotiations—filled with hostility and fear. As the anxiety increased around me, I made an effort to be a conscientious objector and remain neutral. When the Guild strongly suggested membership withhold bylines from stories and hand out subscription cancellation forms to the general public, I tried to diplomatically decline. The negativity of the place only increased. When we were *asked* to wear management-mocking slogan buttons at the newsroom, I refused. When I was *told* to wear a bright shiny button that read: "No Raw Deal" or "Management's Health Plan is Sick" I chose to post a computer screen saver that offered, "Civilized Justice, Compassionate Wisdom, Global Peace."

In music, counter-rhythms can work to produce harmony. In daily life, something has to give. I tired of trying to just write good stories and ignore the office politics. I was disheartened by thinly veiled disdain from co-workers. One afternoon, two guild members dropped by my workstation to mention that a rival paper was hiring in case I was interested. Sigh.

The good news (pun intended) is that even as I silently struggled with my colleagues, the stage was being set for my next, and positive phase—teaching. In September 2002, I had begun to teach hand drumming for a before-school program at Wilson Elementary School in Kenosha. This made for interesting dynamics at home—I taught from 7 to 8 a.m. and somehow my own children still made it to school on time. I agreed to the arrangement because my family worked with me and it seemed like a worthy investment of energy.

So far, my experience as a hand drum instructor had been limited to a few classes of beginner adults. At Wilson I discovered I was not the teacher but the student. The first class consisted of six children, ages 6 through 10, including two sets of rather argumentative siblings. I came in with good intentions and a basic program and sometimes left wondering why I had been there at all. Still, between arguments over who would start a song or get to play the bell, these students created some incredible music, inspired songs and complex rhythms of their own.

A great day would be 10 minutes of really good music. One boy might begin to play a plastic bucket and coffee can (after fighting with his brother for it), setting a strong beat for the others. His sister would come in on a bead-covered shaker and the others filled in with a Rumba beat they had learned from me. Around us, the entire school would begin to file into the gym for breakfast before the school day. The other students' eyes lit up and they rushed over to ask if they could come to drum class too.

The Wilson drummer experience hit a high point in February 2003. Our class was asked to showcase its talents in front of the entire school as part of a Black History Month program. I had to work at the paper that day but took off as soon as I was able, arriving just in time to set up the drums and help the students perform the program's "grand finale." Despite the fact that these kids had been unable to get along during class, the six of them managed to play songs that received an all-school applause. It happened not because these kids had learned songs precisely, but because they had learned how to work together and watch my cues. They had become a drum troupe and I had become a facilitator. Arthur would have been pleased.

The Wilson group taught me that if I wanted to *teach* drumming I had to keep *learning*. The drum program had to be interesting but not frustrating. I watched videos on hand drum teaching methods and brought in instruments from home. Some days I just let the kids create rhythms that had nothing to do with what I had thought I wanted to teach them.

Watching the Wilson kids bask in the admiration of their peers I realized certain things had become true for me regarding drumming: 1) drumming *is* good for people; 2) I might need to be the one to introduce this stuff to these kids. As a result, I began to think it might be time to reconsider a long-forgotten calling to teach.

I had wanted to be a teacher in fact long before I became an overpaid newspaper reporter. Years after telling my mother I wanted to be a writer when I grew up, I thought teaching might be a good thing to do while I wrote in my spare time. I was talked out of this decision by my mother—a former sixth grade teacher—and my best friend. I was about 16 years old at the time and they informed me that I would make a bad teacher because I was too shy. So, being the "gotta please everybody" daughter and friend, I abandoned the idea and chose journalism instead.

Of course, at age 16 I *would* have been a bad teacher. I wasn't ready to be a good teacher for another 30 years. But, just as Emmit was always a runner, I was eventually going to become a teacher. It just took a lot of life experience and a little drum facilitation to get there.

I began to think seriously about teaching in spring, 2003 as tensions with the Guild were at a high. Pondering a change, I looked to drumming but sensed that Kenosha did not need a full-time rhythm circle facilitator any more than I was ready to be one. I looked to other places of work that would feed my soul, or at least not tear it down. The word "potential" came to mind and along with it two environments that have always represented potential for me: libraries and schools. Just entering one or the other has always made me feel like I was coming home—to a place of ideas, future, hope. I chose schools because I had recently had a taste of working with kids and drums. I knew I was leaving the world of adults who acted like children to embrace the intense-but-usually-honest energy of schoolchildren.

Kids will be kids. The author shows a small djembe to curious preschoolers at Pleasant Prairie Renaissance School, spring 2001.

Office politics aside, it was just time for me to leave professional journalism. I had written enough about other people's lives. I was tired of the effort it took to coax people's stories from them, then mold the facts into a readable, happily-ever-after—or not—tale. It was time to live my life, and eventually write it, too.

On April 10, 2003, I officially left the *Kenosha News* to begin adventures in teaching and drumming and drum facilitation and life without "Guild guilt." Ironically, (and probably karmically) two weeks after I left, the *Kenosha News* union and management resolved their 18-month contract dispute (without redressing part-timer needs).

The teachers who set me on the course of teaching were all of the above, with a little help from some song lyrics by folk/pop singer Jewel Kilcher. As often happens, songs take on significance when heard at crucial moments in our lives. During the decision-making process leading to my resignation from the paper, I found myself listening over and over to one of the songs by Jewel from her 1996 compact disc, *Spirit.* The song, "Life Uncommon" tells of a person's conviction in standing tall for her choices against oppressors. The song spoke to *my* spirit—giving me both a sense of strength and a sense of peace with my chosen path. It was my battle cry, minus the battle, because, after all, I am a pacifist.

Re-reading the CD's liner notes, I found Jewel had dedicated "Life Uncommon" to a friend who, she wrote, was a beloved teacher and inspiration. Such is the power of the circle.

Each of us has many "grains of sand" in our proverbial oyster beds. These are negative elements that goad us, dare us to be our better selves. While it is simple to thank the wonderful influences in our lives, it is also so very important to remember the others, too.

Chapter 9

Full Circle: Our Extended
Family of Rhythm

Intricately woven into this journey to magic and music are those who have become close friends through drumming. These are people who could have come only to drum circle events, those who did not have to form extra alliances with us, but chose us as we chose them. Consider this chapter, if you will, "Acknowledgements Part II."

As we opened our home and developed connections with the "percussively curious" in our community, Roger and I began to explore avenues of strengthening connections within this new tribe. We created an electronic newsletter, an *e'zine* we named *Rhythm and News*. For a model we (again) looked to Tom Gill who had developed an electronic newsletter to keep his Milwaukee community apprised of rhythm-based events. Accordingly, I began posting our drum circle schedule along with select drum doings in Milwaukee and northern Illinois. Our local community grew as we honored requests to list items for groups including professional African drummers, Middle Eastern dancers and folks hosting meditation and yoga events.

When we reached a "critical mass" of regulars, we began generating events for our group, such as "a walking drum circle" for Kenosha's annual Civic Veteran's Parade (the Sunday closest to July 4). We also organized "drum safaris"—field trips to exotic drum stores and percussion-based performances in Milwaukee and Chicago.

In 2002, to commemorate the anniversary of my drum baptism, we decided to host a New Year's Day drum event in Kenosha. In keeping with my New Year's Day 2000 drumming experience, we decided to hold a lakeside celebration. The idea was to welcome the New Year—not with booze at midnight, but with rhythm at the civilized time of 12, noon. Yes, it would be out of doors, next to (but not inside!) Southport Beach House. We stressed to the curious: it was guaranteed to be different.

The first New Year's Day Arctic Circle Drumming included Roger, me, Kathy Carson and Karen and Jessica Smith. With the wind blowing from the west, we were sheltered by the 100-old yellow brick bathhouse. We looked to the lake and played improvised rhythms on synthetic-headed drums, five-gallon buckets and pebble-filled Easter egg shakers. This drum circle was, as were those at our home, "unfacilitated." Neither I, nor Roger, took control of the music; it just happened.

Each year since, a growing contingent of hardy (and hearty!) people meet by the lakefront at noon on New Year's Day. Sometimes there have been as many as 17 people—people who read the notice in the paper and bring their small children or others, like Walt, an older neighbor, who came to play on a tube-shaped potato chip container with a cardboard mallet. Some have compared our winter lakeside concerts to the "Polar Bear Swimmers"—folks who dash en masse into the lake each New Year's Day. I like to respond: "We're crazy too, but *we* keep our clothes on!"

Seriously, however, why *do* we do this? In part, it is just to say we did it. It is also a way of being a community—doing something unusual and fun for the sake of being together.

Among those who attend these events is a core of people who have become like family. Some of our new "family" members found us at drum circles we facilitated. Shirley Scheckler and Greg Yanasek, for example, met us as they attended a drum circle at the 2001 Health and Wellness Expo at the University of Wisconsin-Parkside.

John and Jennifer Von Eiff heard us before they saw us. In late summer, 2002, Roger and I were leading a circle for an annual art fair held at a nature sanctuary in Kenosha called Hawthorne Hollow. John recalls, "I could hear these drums in the woods and thought the natives were restless." Curious, John and Jen came to watch our 15-person group play drums, tambourines and bells. They also picked up a flyer of information about Rhythm in the Round.

Not long after this, Shirley, John and Jennifer signed up for a hand drum class I was teaching at the local university. It was their first drum class and my first experience teaching at the university. What we didn't realize was that it was also the first time the university had agreed to offer a hand drum class there. Someone in Facilities Scheduling apparently did not grasp the concept that a class titled "Hand Drum for Fun" could mean that the 12-inch African-style drums might in fact need to be played at some time during the course.

My four adult students and I were assigned to room D11, Molinaro Hall, a regular classroom next to other regular classrooms in which professors were presenting Colonial American History and Psychology 101. About seven minutes into the first class of the six-week course, we were asked to "tone it down." Shirley, John, Jennifer and another student named Candy and I packed up our drums and began what became a weekly ritual of nomadic wandering with our large, and largely unwelcome, drums. It took five phone calls and five weeks but university staff finally hit upon a novel idea: maybe I should hold class inthe music room.

Inconvenient as this was for all involved, our misadventures forged a bond between us. By the second or third week of campus trekking we had become a tribe. En route back to the parking lot after class one evening, Shirley announced she was getting married and asked if Roger and I would provide music and a drum circle for the ceremony.

By the end of that session of classes, Shirley, John and Jennifer began attending our monthly drum circle. If we gave gold stars for drum event attendance, John and Jennifer would have pages of them. (This is particularly appropriate as Jennifer is an elementary school teacher.) Since 2002, they have attended nearly every one of our home circles (Jennifer usually bringing hot snacks!), joined us for musical workshops on the didjeridu and Tibetan throat-singing, helped with music during a radio interview (whose host turned out to be rather cynical), drummed in parades and never miss the chance to drum with us in sub-arctic weather on New Year's Day.

Each month, as we introduce ourselves at our home circles, John likes to note that since meeting us he and Jennifer have done "many weird things." But we notice they are the first to ask about the next "drum safari" or workshop adventure!

Opening our house to strangers was a big step for Roger and for us as a couple. Presenting ourselves as a family has also, I believe, attracted the energies of other family- and couple-oriented drummers. Offering our home to strangers, we were and are offering a place where people can bond as a village or tribe.

Only once in five years has the connection been more negative than positive. A 20-something man e-mailed me to ask about drumming. We invited him to a circle but when he came to our home he was restless and seemed agitated. A few months later he e-mailed again to ask me to remove him from the mailing list. He said he wouldn't be returning to our circle because he felt he had "been made to feel unwelcome."

This was a sad thing for me to hear, but I knew we had not done anything that could have been read as offensive. We offer instruments, a place to explore them and support and encouragement. With that, we figure people can and should take responsibility for their own good time. This person, it appeared, wanted someone—us perhaps—to tell him exactly what he needed to be happy.

I could have deleted his message and his e-mail address but chose instead to send him a simple thought. I wrote back, "It would seem that you were looking for something we could not provide. I hope in the future you find a circle that meets your needs."

This young man was the exception to the rule. Most of those who discover our home tend to come back and stay a while. Some of our tribal elders now include:

Tom Anger (who taught himself how to make didjeridus from plastic tubes in his mid-70s and helped in the production of photos for this book), Tom's wife Mercedes, a massage therapist and energy healer; Jeanne Reeb, (a New Year's Day Arctic Circle regular); Melanie Hovey, who had us host a Mardi Gras drum circle at Lemon Street Gallery and hired me to facilitate at her parent's 25th wedding anniversary; her husband Steve, (who doesn't drum much but has been there when we needed help moving a 4-ton boulder on our front lawn); and Ed Soler, who came to our 2005 New Year's Day drumming after playing drums all night for a rock band.

And yes, many more: Wilhelm and his wacky "found sounds"; Meryle, the massage therapist who plays a mean double bell; and Ed who discovered a talent for carving Native American flutes after hearing Roger play.

Many of the Kenosha drum clan posing for a pre-parade photo, June 2002.

Mickey Hart, former drummer for the Grateful Dead and "world beat" percussionist, speculates about the strong bond between drum-minded people in his book *Drumming to the Edge of Magic: A Journey into the Spirit of Percussion.* In the excerpt below, Hart describes the closeness of this connection:

> It is hard to pinpoint the exact moment when I awoke to the fact that my tradition— rock and roll—did have a spirit side, that there was a branch of the family that had maintained the ancient connection between the drum and the gods. I suppose it was a little like meeting some long lost cousins and realizing with a start that these are your relatives, that you are rhythmically related, and in drumming that's the same as blood.

Discovering we had a rhythmically related extended family was no small thing for Roger and me. Roger comes from a family of several siblings, aunts, uncles and cousins, so no pressing need to seek out more family. At the other end of the spectrum, mine was a two-sib family with no cousins that had managed just fine in our small-group sort of way. Together, Roger and I found that as the drum called people to our *house*, it also invited them to become part of our *home*. It has changed the way we look at gifts and how we celebrate major holidays—our house is a gift to others; they in turn come back with unexpected offerings of musical energy, assistance and "Cheese in a Can" for special occasions! I didn't know I needed more family, but am happy to have found these new and interesting drum siblings!

For Rhythm in the Round this is coming full circle, because this is why we started on the path in the first place. When I came home with that borrowed drum on Dec. 19, 1999, it occurred to me that this was an instrument that would sound better if other people were playing with me. I would not have stuck with the drum or become this involved had it not been for the interest, support and friendship of other people. At the end of facilitated circles, I like to say, "Thank you all so much, because, I *really* can't make this music without you!"

Chapter 10

Worlds of Facilitation

I had such fun at Walk in the Woods, it brought back memories of my favorite part of music class in grade school. I have purchased Arthur Hull's book so while I can't have the circle start as soon as I hoped, I'll be better prepared...I've also discovered websites from other drum circles and may try some of those while waiting to get ours going...Thank you so much for your advice and more importantly inspiration. I am really grateful to have discovered an old past time made possible in the "grown-up" days. Your enthusiasm and passion really come through and that is a great gift...

–Carolyn (later known as Ambriel)

I am sending you a big THANK YOU for sending me the information about (Tom Gill's) class...I did attend and I experienced the most amazing two hours!...I am 59 years old and cannot read a note of music, but felt so comfortable as a contributing member of the group/community...I also think this may be another new beginning for me!

–Phyllis

When I receive notes like these I wonder: "What did I do? I don't remember saying or doing anything special..." I am beginning to recognize it's not what we do, but an elusive, yet tangible reaction many people have to their first exposures to drumming with a group. Carolyn and Phyllis and many like them are expressing this reaction as Passion with a capital P! Pondering this passion I realize that it's not me (or even Tom or Arthur) but the drums—the drums facilitate the magic and magic is the key ingredient here.

For those of us called to facilitate, the objective is much more subtle than we think it is. It is not about what rhythms we teach or the music we help a group create, but how we facilitate this Passion to engage with the drum and with each other. This subtle task is what we call "facilitating from the side." It happens when we help someone find the perfect drum voice, or support someone in our circle who has decided to start a drum circle of his or her own.

We who have just begun to walk the path of teacher and/or facilitator often find ourselves in the position of guide or mentor. It happens so quickly that our first reaction may be, "But I'm not an expert!" It is scary to be asked to advise, but as Arthur has been heard to say, "Teach what you know."

I began to teach what I knew sooner than I thought I knew anything. The first questions popped up at my first gigs—children at the Boys and Girls Club and the caregivers of preschoolers at those daycare facilities. As soon as I arrived some place with a drum and a bucket of sound makers, the questions began: "How do you make these things?" and "How did you get involved in drumming" and "Where can I buy a good drum?" We don't always "know what we know" until someone asks. I would look at my scraggly collection of things and just start telling my story—not just how and what I had collected, but *why*. This book is the long version of those answers.

One who asked for direct guidance in organizing drum gatherings was Lorraine Achey. I met Lorraine in October 2000 at Barry Bernstein's weekend retreat. Before the weekend was over, Lorraine and I had begun a friendship with a "sisters-of-the-drum" flavor. She lives in Kansas and I live in Wisconsin so we started an e-mail and "snail mail" correspondence. Our friendship soon evolved into the exchange of uniquely percussive gifts. One month she sent me a box that rattled. Inside were four pot lids of various sizes. These, said the enclosed note, were "Lid-a-phones" that when struck with wooden spoons (also included) produced different notes in scale. She wrote that she had raided garage sales far and wide after discovering a brand of cast aluminum last made in the 1970s with tonal qualities rivaling those of expensive, real musical gongs.

In return I sent her a box of rhythm shakers made from plastic and copper toilet tank floats I had filled with beach pebbles and unpopped popcorn kernels. These, I informed her, were my non-patented "Flo-Shakers" based on an idea I had gotten from Tom Gill.

A few months, later Lorraine embarked on teaching drum classes and hosting a monthly women's drum circle in her hometown of Pittsburg, Kansas. E-mails shared excitement about her latest percussion finds in junk stores and the best books on conga drum rhythms. When she was asked to conduct a rhythm circle for developmentally disabled children, she wrote me for advice.

Rhythm Sister Lorraine is one of those people who can make just about anything with their hands and find pleasure in doing so. Her talents range from origami checkbook covers to quilted jackets for her puppies and bags for hand drums. Not having such skills or inclination, I am always a good test consumer for her latest creations, particularly when they run to the drum-related. In the summer of 2004, en route to visiting my (biologically related) sister in Arkansas, I stopped in Joplin, Missouri to spend some time with Lorraine. I had not even washed my face after the 10-hour drive when Lorraine rushed into the motel room with two drums she had made from cardboard tubes and vinyl pool liner. We spent much of the evening discussing the musical merits of her "sonodrums" and swapping rhythms like the middle part to Calypso and a beginner pattern called "Mama Pappa," which we discovered sound particularly good together.

As I left for Arkansas, Lorraine presented me with an origami card she had made with a note, "Thanks for providing me with so much useful info and encouragement with drumming." I didn't know I was doing much except playing some favorite rhythms with a friend. I guess I was "facilitating from the side."

My next stop that summer was a visit to my sister Fraser, who lives in Fayetteville, Arkansas. Six years my junior, Fraser has disabilities that have limited the types interests we have in common. On a previous visit, I had shown Fraser some of my drums and she expressed interest in playing them. This time when I brought out the drums we just started playing together. She learned a few patterns then made up her own that complemented and enhanced mine.

Today Fraser is building her own percussion collection and requests ethnic-based percussion music as Christmas gifts. Playing drums with my sister gave me a glimpse of a skill I did not know she had; she in turn discovered a creative outlet she never knew existed. I contend that this was not something I did—I may have facilitated from the side—the drums did all the rest.

My sister Fraser playing on a drum made by my "rhythm sister" Lorraine, during a summer visit in 2004.

In the summer of 2003 drums facilitated magic when a man came into our basement telling us he'd heard about our circle in a national drumming magazine. Dan said he'd read an article on drum circles in the June/July edition of *Drum!*, a magazine originally geared to the interests of drumset-type drummers. I recalled I had responded to a questionnaire about our drum circle but it did not occur to me that the information would wind up in this magazine. Rhythm in the Round's Second Saturday Circle had been listed in an article titled "Drum Circle: Find Your Tribe Directory." This was part of a feature discussing the rise of drum circles in the U.S. Our Kenosha circle was one of only four posted for the entire state of Wisconsin—the others were Tom's in Wauwatosa, one in Madison and one in Oshkosh.

It turned out that Dan lived only a ten-minute drive from our house. He became a regular at our circles, began collecting high-quality djembes and taught himself the complex skills of hand drum tuning and repair. In 2004, when we took a short break from hosting the home circle, Dan decided to start his own in the large, heated garage of his parent's home. "I needed my drum fix so I thought I'd start a drum circle at my house," he said. With that he chose a name—Fanner's Drum Circles—and had business cards made advertising his circle and drum repair services.

Dan's move from owning a couple hand drums to sharing personal space with community drummers validated the path Roger and I had taken in the spring of 2000. When we started playing hand drums, there were no drum circles to be found for 60 miles—four years later there were two, two miles apart.

For me "facilitation" has become a metaphor for a way of life. As a substitute teacher in the public schools, I have found that I facilitate every time I step into the classroom. In the past two years I have discovered that substitute teaching and drum circle facilitation are really just different expressions of the same gig. In both environments I am dealing with a host of unknowns. In the classroom my instruments are books and lesson plans and the "group song," with luck, is a lesson of some sort. The challenge found in both is to establish some kind of rhythm so we can get on with the job of mental or musical creativity.

Sometimes my assignment is not as lead teacher, but to support the work and lessons presented by another teacher. As I help keep the lid on unruly behavior, or re-read directions for a math assignment to an individual student, I realize I am playing a support rhythm; facilitating from the side.

Unlike regular teachers, substitute teachers often find that the lessons of the day are not usually ones the usual teacher had in mind. This is because we may have to calm down a class of 16 kindergarteners before we can get to teaching them about "words that end in the word 'an'."

Not long into subbing, I figured out why students of all ages get so wound up when they encounter a substitute teacher. They are afraid. As a whole, substitute teachers represent an unknown and therefore something to be feared. In the animal kingdom, fear represents weakness. Students, like all good animals, cover their insecurities by regressing to behavior ranging from unfocused to uncivilized. In the split second after entering a classroom, the cry goes up from the pack, "We've got a sub! Awww riiight!!!" Before they even take their seats (probably not theirs) they have already decided: 1) The sub doesn't know who they are 2) The sub doesn't know how to teach what they are learning 3) It is time for mass hysteria and prolonged chaos.

To offset these handicaps I began to make it my top priority to set a tone of safety and security in every classroom village I visit. To establish this I attempt two things: help at least one student solve some kind of problem and learn names. If a substitute teacher assists a single student with the answer to a question (it helps if it's something you can answer), the message is communicated to other students that maybe the class can be survived after all.

As for learning names, I cannot endorse this strongly enough. It can be hard—particularly if you have groups of 25 kids that change every 40 minutes—but it worth the effort. If I know I won't be able to get them all, I strive to learn the names of one or two good kids and, of course, any of the potential troublemakers. You can use cues like listening for someone to call their name or read it off of their paper. In elementary school, students often have name cards taped to their desks.

In classrooms and in drum circles, learning and remembering names conveys respect. It says that you care; you make an effort to recognize the individuality of a person and this—whether acknowledged or not—is a sacred connection between people. It is also one that is becoming a scarce resource in the world today. As a bonus, when a substitute teacher learns and remembers a few names, students think he or she has magic powers— an illusion definitely worth cultivating!

Additionally, I have discovered that the cross pollination of teacher and facilitator is more than just a metaphor—on any given day I find myself using circle-type facilitation techniques in the classroom. One day I was supposed to teach science to alternative learners—high school students whose behavior or intellectual development labeled them at risk for academic achievement. The lesson plan indicated we were to review the concept of "Experiments and Scientific Method," but my students chose instead to start the class by refereeing a lover's spat between two classmates. After having the unhappy couple removed from the room, I knew I had to do something to retrieve the class's scattered attention and settle the frenzied atmosphere in the room.

I had about 20 minutes of time to fill and a room of students on high energy. A herd of loud drums would have been a really good thing to have about then. Lacking these, I chose to demonstrate the Scientific Method by conducting an on-the-spot science experiment with what materials I could find in the not-a-science-lab classroom.

Inspired by some sugar substitute that had spilled on my desk, I scooped it onto a piece of paper and presented it to the students and said, "We are going to observe this substance I just found, make some hypotheses about it and experiment with it to determine what it is." In the next few minutes, I had them try different things with the sugar and compare it to a piece of chalk I ground up. I wanted to dissolve both in water, but as there was no sink, we used water from the teacher's coffee pot. And because there were no tools, I had to step on the chalk, after which I joked that I had just contaminated the sample but it was still OK. I was going for the concept that to find out what something is, we can try experiments with a control, or a substance we already know. Lucky for me, we ran out of time just as I ran out of my entertaining and scientifically improbable materials.

In drum circle terms we could say what I did in those 20 minutes was "adjust the song" at a point where the music had unraveled. We may not have created a musical masterpiece (or solved any of the great mysteries of science) but using diversion and a bit of humor, I had helped restore the rhythm of my restless students.

Of all the skills needed to be an effective teacher or rhythm facilitator, adaptability, as previously mentioned, is perhaps most vital. In one week I danced through a gym with four-year-olds waving colored scarves, taught the formula for the circumference of a circle to learning disabled eighth graders (after quickly relearning it myself of course) and lectured on the skills of résumé writing to high school students. And when in doubt (which is often), I pull out my Substitute Secret Weapon: a videotape of STOMP, a group that uses everything except musical instruments to create song and dance. Whatever mayhem may be taking place in the classroom comes to a screeching halt as students sit and "shush" each other, mesmerized by young men and women making music by bouncing basketballs, shaking car keys and banging on pots, pans and garbage cans. Not only does this engage their attention and diffuse disruptive behavior, but sometimes STOMP becomes what parents and educators call a "teachable moment," one in which I can point out how our interests and hobbies can become careers in the real world.

The key here is *connection*. In all worlds of facilitation, the teacher or facilitator must find a way to connect to his or her circle. Usually this is by watching and listening to those in the circle. An important lesson in connecting to the circle was taught to me in October 2004 by a group of 15 elderly persons in various stages of Alzheimer's disease.

Until this time, my format consisted of starting circles with the "element of surprise"—having people play instruments before I said anything. On this particular day, before going to the Alzheimer's facility I rethought this approach. It occurred to me that unlike most groups, people with Alzheimer's disease live in a world that is often confusing to them. They may have lost the ability to remember family names or even their own name. More significantly, they may be aware that they cannot remember things that were once very important to them. The last thing people like this need, I realized, was another surprise. With this in mind, I knew this program would be different.

Arriving at the Beverly Health Care facility in Kenosha, I first introduced each instrument slowly and gently to the assembled group of elders. Each person took something to play and soon we had a song of sorts. One woman created a distinctive beat that sounded like "1, 2, 3 and 4" and we all began to chant this together. Proud of her contribution, she smiled brightly and began to sing it louder—in German.

As the circle continued I said something I had never thought of before. I told them that while they played they might recall a song from long ago because our bodies remember things even when our minds do not. This was something that came from my head, but mostly from my heart, in the intention to connect to these people in a way that was meaning-filled.

Arthur calls the things we say to groups between songs "windows of communication." Sometimes a facilitator uses these windows to explain the playing technique or origin of an instrument or present a metaphor that links the drum circle experience with everyday life. For me, windows of communication have become bridges between me and my circles and schoolroom classes. The more I connect to those I am with, the more at ease I am with my new—and true—calling.

Hand in hand with the concept of facilitating from the side is another of Arthur's adages, "Facilitate and get out of the way." The concept is, ideally, what all parents, teachers and rhythm facilitators aspire to do. This type of facilitating is about giving advice when asked and nurturing natural gifts, then letting nature take its course. As a budding facilitator and teacher, facilitating and getting out of the way was the best thing my teachers could have done for me. Teachers Arthur and Tom were instructive to a point— after that point, I was on my own to learn, to make mistakes and to learn from those mistakes.

As we facilitate from the side we also learn not to take things personally. There will be days when members of our circle are not ready for the lesson at hand. They may be bored, distracted or even in pain. It's usually not about us, or what we know, and that's OK.

At the end of the day, we are all facilitators—in the classroom, in the rhythm circle, at work, with our children and with our spouses. Over the years I have been repeatedly surprised to find out that facilitation goes both ways. In that first phone call with Tom, I was struck by his attention to my questions and drum quest. His comments led me to believe that even in my non-knowledge of drumming I had a perspective that enhanced his own drum path. I have been honored when asked my opinion on materials for homemade instruments or tricks in keeping young children interested in their drum lessons. When our teachers tell us that they are still learning too, it keeps us students from fearing failure.

The energy and inspiration of making music with others does not belong to me, or Arthur, or Mickey or Tom but can and should be *facilitated* by everyone who is in a position to do so. Unlike traditional corporate or commercial enterprises, the work of community drumming and rhythm circles is not about competition. It is about cooperation. It is not about vying with fellow facilitators for gigs—it is about sharing the magic of rhythmic connection with everyone who expresses a desire for it.

Whatever you do, wherever you do it, the important thing is that you *do*—that you *do* choose to teach and share as much as you can.

Chapter 11

Do Try This At Home—
And Everywhere Else!

- I am not from a village in West Africa.
- I do not have a degree in music therapy.
- Rhythm in the Round is not a religion.

These are not apologies, but statements of fact. Amending the above:

- I am not from Africa, but I have a love of African drums and rhythms.
- I am not a music therapist, but what we do together with rhythm IS therapeutic.
- Rhythm in the Round is not a religion, but it *is* spiritual.

Amazingly, some of us who call ourselves rhythm circle facilitators have been criticized for efforts to share drumming culture. In a telephone conversation with someone I had not met face-to-face, I was roundly dressed down. "How dare you take drums to people when you are not an African teacher?" she queried. "Why don't you spend your time studying with (Milwaukee-based teachers from Senegal and Mali)?"

I replied: "I know I will never be a master djembe player raised in an African village, but I can and do promote an appreciation of African drums. I can learn about them, pass on some of the drum's heritage and share an enthusiasm for playing them."

I also do not believe that non-ethnic facilitators denigrate African traditions: the teachers and facilitators I know make a sincere effort to learn authentic playing techniques and rhythms, usually from traditional teachers. I for one would never presume to say I teach "ethnically specific" drumming, but I do like to present a culturally based song or two during the course of a six-week drum class. If I present the song "Fanga," I do it with reverence: I'll preface the lesson by giving students the story behind the song, adding that our version of it is not meant to replicate "Fanga" as played in villages of West Africa. Because we live in a different culture our interpretation of the rhythm will naturally be different.

For students desiring "the next level" of ethnically specific expertise I eagerly share the names of those in our area originally from West Africa, which at this time includes Oumar Sagna and Lucky Diop.

Perhaps some of those who criticize are afraid that open community circles such as ours somehow dilute or disrespect the root culture of drumming. Tactfully, I respond that we non-ethnic facilitators truly believe we are offering something good to people. I note that we offer an exposure to a culture of drumming in an atmosphere of equality unavailable to many people today.

This "offering something good" is why we come together in the first place. The people who come to our living room or basement or gather in parks are (generally) not there to become "African djembe masters." They come because they want to express themselves creatively using musical instruments. It is as simple and as beautiful as that. As I told my critic, "I would rather offer people a place to play together than not do it because it wasn't culturally specific."

THIS is why we do this! Above, a bunch of us, making great music at the post-Arctic Circle jam in the Poyner's living room, New Year's Day 2002.

The issue of ethnic purity is one aspect of public misunderstanding about drumming in this country today. Community drumming, particularly in the Midwest, is a relatively new phenomenon. It is not surprising that as it emerges into mainstream consciousness, there is disagreement among providers about what it should be. But in general, such confusion is a moot issue: drum circles can be many things and should be just "let be." If we live in a free society (as we are led to believe), then we should be free to hold drum events for whatever reasons—or no reason whatsoever.

Over the years I have had calls asking if our drum circles are pagan, just for women or Native American. They can be, but mostly they are not. Our home circles, and many of the circles we host in parks and at fairs, have no agenda and are open to all for the pure enjoyment of playing music.

There are of course occasions in life that call for specific direction. Drum circles are often offered to particular populations, such as the well elderly or Girl Scouts. They are also used in celebration, protest and grieving. At times like these drumming takes on an intention and a direction. As a drum circle provider, it is an honor—and humbling—to be invited to help people mark their mother's 80th birthday, dad's retirement from a lifetime career, or communal tragedies like 911 or the conflict in Iraq. And if someone asks if I do a woman-specific circle, the answer is also "yes." If an event needs a specific direction, the intention can be set for it.

We have had people ask if drum circles are a type of religion. To this I like to say, "No, but they are spiritual." Whenever several people drum and play rhythm together, something powerful happens at levels both individual and communal. That power does not need to have a name. Naming or labeling our drumming experience can lead to artificial divisions; the real deal with group drumming is not division, it is unity.

I've also found it's not good enough just to say, "We aren't a religion." Trying to explain that "it's all good" sometimes gets me into hot water with religious fundamentalists who slam me with a "godless heathen" label. For anyone who believes that every culture should follow the same religious path, group drumming may represent a willful deviation from their perception of truth. Once a woman asked me if I was worried that drums might attract people who aren't Christian. Suppressing an inclination to say, "Who cares?" I replied that even if that were the case we would still make good music together.

The common denominator among many who do not understand drum circles is fear of the unknown. Interestingly, sometimes those who aspire to share drums are also afraid. On one occasion I was asked by a facilitator colleague to conduct a circle of young children. Shortly before the event I received an e-mail from this man instructing me to: "Please be sure to avoid any reference to anything spiritual." OK, I thought. I realized that this particular facilitator was afraid I would do some type of "drum voodoo" and did not see that most people would find it inappropriate to promote spiritual stuff to 6- to 12-year olds attending summer camp. What he also failed to get was that the word "spirit" is just another word for "energy" and when you've got kids and drums you can bet those kids will put a lot of spirit into their playing no matter what the facilitator does or says.

Another point of contention is occasional tension between people formally trained as music therapists and laypeople offering up a hands-on musical experience. I do what I do because I think it is good for people *because* we have seen the good that can happen through group drumming. The concept is to share percussion toys and let intuition guide the outcome for facilitator and participants alike. It may not follow a specified medical protocol and it may not be music therapy as some know it, but we know at core that it is very therapeutic.

My journey to the drum and to drumming with others has been intimately linked to my own health and wellness. Drumming came into my awareness during recovery from minor surgery. Significant medical issues since then have all had some type of drum connection.

One such occurrence took place in early May 2002 when several facilitators and I invited Barry Bernstein to Milwaukee to conduct a weekend of workshops. On Saturday night I got out of my car and felt excruciating pain in my right leg. Although I could barely drive, I continued to the dance event where I lay on the floor while musicians and dancers swirled overhead. The next day I was committed to facilitate a drum circle at the annual WomanSpirit Faire in Racine. Still unable to walk, I hopped around playing my cedar flute to engage people in music making. Two days later I discovered that I had in fact torn the muscles in my leg and was looking at a five-week recovery. Four weeks later I was up and around so I could facilitate a 65-student circle at my daughter's school.

For the sake of drumming and facilitating, I also underwent elective surgery on my left elbow. In June 2003, I had a procedure to release a tendon in my elbow that was cramping my drumming style and making it difficult to haul around a vanload of drums. Four days later, Roger drove me to a drum circle where I beat a djun djun with a stick in my good hand and my other arm in a cast. Having that surgery was the best thing I could have done for my elbow but I wouldn't have bothered about it if I hadn't wanted to keep drumming.

These anecdotes illustrate that when we wholeheartedly love something that is intrinsically wholesome, it can make us spiritually healthier. At a time when many women my age find their metabolism slowing down, mine has picked up the pace. Where some struggle with memory loss, I go into a classroom and memorize 20 names in about 20 minutes (until the kids put on their coats and then I have to start all over). As others lose their get-up-and go I am told at the end of an hour's drum circle, "Your energy is just amazing."

Some of our friends report that the activity of drumming has mitigated some of the symptoms of conditions that affect them including diabetes and emphysema. Others say they just feel more energetic since they discovered the drum. I may not have the documented medical proof for it, but I know there is healing type energy in the drums for the people who play on them.

In the past ten years there have been studies documenting connections between rhythm and health—among them memory improvement in Alzheimer's patients, immune system strengthening and rehabilitation from drug use. Psychologists, medical doctors and physical therapists are finding patients benefiting from playing and hearing drums, didjeridus, gongs and tuning forks. Percussive pioneers include Barry Bitman, Lawrence Friedman, Barry Bernstein, Judy Piazza, Phil Jones, Mickey Hart, Lee Veal and Ubaka Hill. With very few exceptions, most of those named above are not formally trained music therapists. But each knows that rhythm has amazing healing powers.

Those not quite sold on the therapeutic nature of drumming might ask the mother of John (whose name has been changed for his privacy), a 14-year-old boy with autism. One evening in 2003 I was doing a drum circle with John and classmates. I demonstrated "call and response"—an exercise in which a person taps out a rhythm on a cowbell and everyone copies the beat on his or her drum. Many of John's middle school-age peers were trying so hard to be cool they had declined to participate in the activity. When it came to John's turn he eagerly took the cowbell and a few kids exchanged looks implying they didn't expect much from this student who never spoke a word in school. To everyone's surprise—and my great pleasure—John whacked out some very cool rhythms. After each one, he waited just the right length of time for the group to answer. John hit the bell and 45 of his peers answered him with a thunder of drumbeats. He gave a huge smile and did it again. For a very brief time, the bell had become John's voice, a way to connect to his classmates.

Drum doubters could also ask the opinion of staff at an Alzheimer's adult daycare facility in Kenosha. As I left one of my regular visits to St. Joe's, a staff member said, "After drumming we get smiles from guys here who don't smile much any more."

Are smiles on the proscribed list of music therapies? Probably not, but you can be sure that John's mom and the nursing home staff believe smiling is a good thing and that just maybe drumming has something to do with it.

The bottom line is this: If you think drumming is good for you, then do it. If you think it is something you need to share with friends and family, do so. Do not let yourself get hung up on negatives: "I am not Native American," or "I can't read a note of music," or even "I don't have any instruments." If it sounds good to you, then the goodness of drumming in community will come to you. If you open your doors (or find a church basement to rent), you may find friends showing up with instruments they found at garage sales and life stories of wonder and transformation. I know because it happened to us. Yes, *do* try this at home—and everywhere else!

Chapter 12

Trust the Song

> There is only one rule—don't stop
> playing. Trust that you can make music
> and that we can create a song together.
>
> –Heather Poyner, rhythm facilitator

When we talk about rhythm facilitation, it can sound like something we do *to* people and *to* their music. While yes, some things need doing, like keep small children from hitting one another with sticks, the most important thing we all need to do is *trust*. We—facilitators and drum circle participants— need to trust the circle and ourselves. We need to believe that we can make music together.

It may sound simplistic and saccharine, but trust is really one of those things that make the world, and our circle of drummers, go around. It bears stating because trust does not come easily for many people, particularly in the times in which we live today.

In the previous chapter I mentioned the sometimes-asked question, "Is this (Rhythm in the Round) some kind of religion?" Another way to answer this is, "No, but what we do *is* faith-based." In other words, we couldn't do what we do without faith. It's a leap of faith to sit in a drum circle and a leap of faith to step into the center of that circle. The circle is about faith and trust and that is exactly why I chose it (or it chose me).

Often it is the smallest children who best understand trust. Most children up to the age of 10 will come into a roomful of drums and musical instruments and, if not otherwise stopped, will grab a drum (usually the largest they can find) and just start playing. If there's a stick nearby you can bet they'll apply that to the head of the drum—never mind that it's your favorite goatskin djembe. There might be 20 kids all beating something in a different rhythm, and it doesn't matter to them if the song never has a *one* or a recognizable pattern. They are just doing what comes naturally: they are having fun.

Once this same group of 20 children hits the pre-puberty zone the music will change. There may be some who still play with happy abandon but several will approach the drums hesitantly. By age 15, many just sit there because they are not about to do this thing that this middle-aged woman (as old as their mother only dressed more strangely) is suggesting they do. Either they are too cool or they think the facilitator thinks he or she is too cool—either way, the kids aren't buying it.

Fast forward. Let's bring that group of school children back to the drum circle as 30-something adults. Now these children, who may be parents, attorneys or schoolteachers, come into the room and sit in front of instruments and wait to be told what to do. Some may be curious but decline the offer of an instrument. When the song gets going a few jump in and play, but many will tap hesitantly on a drum or start to play and say, "Oops, I messed up!" and stop playing.

As we grow older many of us find our sense of play has been replaced by the need to be in control. We begin to fear failure and minimize experiences that put us at risk for failing. Put us in front of a bunch of drums and the initial reaction is panic. Adults who may have banged the stuffing out of a drum 20 years ago are now terrified to be asked to touch these drums. Or, if we start, we may freeze up in self-consciousness and stop playing from fear of making a mistake and looking foolish in front of other adults.

Once again, I find the role of teacher and facilitator intersect. Just as my job as a substitute teacher is to set a tone of security for a room of students, it is also my job as a drum facilitator to help people through fear so we can play music together. But it is not enough—or maybe it is too much—to say to a group, "Hey this is easy, anyone can do it!" This might throw folks further into panic mode, "But what if I do it *wrong*?" they wonder. What is needed is *trust*. They need to feel they can make mistakes and nothing dreadful will happen. This means we can take risks. It means taking the chance that maybe we will fail, that maybe the song will crash…AND "It's still OK!"

How do we instill trust in people who no longer trust the world they live in or their ability to be creative? We start by sitting in a circle. We sit in a circle so that one is not the leader, and so we all can learn from one another. In the drum circle, no one is better or worse—there are no first chairs as there are in band and orchestra.

The next step is to remind the group that there are no mistakes, that making spontaneous music is really a grand experiment in which we all get to take part. And sometimes, we simply tell people, "Just keep playing—don't stop. Trust the song." I have found that telling adults to keep playing and trust that music will happen does keep them going. Music really *does* happen.

It could be that doubt makes the music sweeter. I do know the music made after doubting that it could be done is often powerful. It is *empowering.* Our job as facilitators is to nurture gifts already present in each person in the circle. Our function is to astound people—not with our skills, but with their own talents. But first, we have to help people trust themselves and believe they can contribute to the song.

No doubt! A two-year-old boy confidently creates a song on three drums while Mom looks on during Kenosha's Cohorama festival, June 2001.

This trust thing is not a message for just those with whom I work—it is a message I tell myself every time I step into the middle or sit in a circle with others. As a new facilitator, I have had moments in which I stopped a circle dead in its tracks. And I didn't feel like trying it again any time soon. But I did, because I trusted that this was something worth doing, even if it involved risk.

The job of substitute teacher is *loaded* with the need for trust. First, Kenosha Unified School District has to trust me—trust that I am intellectually and physically capable of working with students. The district trusts that I, and my fellow subs, will be able to jump into a situation with minimal or no preparation (assignments coming in at 5:40 a.m. some days) to manage the minds and energies of young learners.

This same trust gets substitute teachers through each day. For the most part we have not studied teachers' manuals for every subject from "Everyday Math" to "The World of Medieval Europe" (and good luck even finding them in the classroom). Yet, we still trust ourselves to produce a positive educational experience each day.

For me, trust is a defining theme of life. As I began putting this book together it dawned on me trust was an important component of journalism and its lack a factor for my departure from the newspaper trade.

People who write for publication have to trust their sources of information. The reading public trusts that an accurate story has been produced. Even so, one of the edicts of journalism is to *never* show a story to a source prior to publication. I understand that the premise of this rule is to prevent the compromise of information. Yet, over the years I sensed that many in the trade had come to believe they knew it all, were always right, or both. Sometimes referred to as "jaded cynicism," this was an attitude I did not want to adopt.

Writing this book, I realize, requires me to do something that I could not do as a professional journalist: share my work ahead of time. Unlike journalism, I will invite my sources to read what I've said about them before we go to press. I'll also ask friends and family to help weed out glaring grammar errors, embarrassing typos and my constant misuse of commas! (Thanks PJ!)

Letting people see my copy ahead of time will take much trust—trust that I can take the opinions of others in the spirit of constructive criticism. Trust that maybe I don't know it all and yes, that other viewpoints are welcome.

Leaving journalism for teaching and rhythm facilitation was a leap of faith, an act of trust in the unknown. Now, every day I must trust others and trust my own instincts.

In the drum circle the song falls apart when those in the circle stop trusting—when we drop our hands and say: "Oops, I keep messing up!" or stop playing because we think others are making "mistakes."

It is the responsibility of *everyone* in the circle to keep the song going because even facilitators can forget to trust. There are times when it can seem it's taking forever for a circle to settle down and get to a musical place. Frustrated, a facilitator may stop trusting the group's ability to create music and work hard to control the song. This often creates confusion and anxiety in the circle. People who had begun to play from the heart all of a sudden are made to feel they are doing it wrong. The result: participants may stop trusting themselves, stop trusting the facilitator and stop playing. End of story, end of circle.

The answer is to keep going. The drum circle is about give and take, and the trust that together we'll find the music, and the music will be good.

Chapter 13

Not Just for Kids, Not Just Drums

Soon after beginning our journey into community drumming, Roger and I discovered we were involved in something so new to our area that it had not yet registered on the social radar of Kenosha. It didn't take long to realize that, because most people had never seen or been a part of a drum circle, it was easy for them to make assumptions about it. Among those assumptions were some or all of the following:

- Drum circles are groups of teenagers on drugs pounding on drums.
- Drum circles are just for little kids.
- Drum circles just have drums.

Having come to drum circles as relatively mature adults, Roger and I were a bit mystified, "What teenagers? What drugs?" Our model for drum circles was one set by Tom and others—responsible adults not on any high-inducing substances except for the natural endorphins naturally generated by drumming.

Thus, we found early attempts to offer drumming to people outside of home circles were sometimes met with reactions ranging from amused curiosity to silent distrust. This of course did not stop us from thinking public circles might be a good idea. In June 2001, I accepted a request to conduct a community drum circle in Kenosha for a lakefront festival called "Cohorama." In addition to a traditional fishing contest (for Coho of course) the fest offered entertainment that included carnival rides and late-night rock bands. The Kenosha Institute of the Arts thought an afternoon drum circle might be an element of wholesome, family fun.

So far, I had conducted circles for specific types of groups of children and adults. I had not as yet taken a bunch of instruments out to the general public with an open invitation to play them. Additionally, this was the very first time that the general public of Kenosha had been exposed to a drum circle of any type. Not knowing what to expect but being game to the idea, Roger and I arrived with a van full of instruments, set up chairs in a circle and began to play.

The first to join the circle were not members of the public but drum friends from Milwaukee and some who had become part of our small living room group on Second Saturdays. As the music began, a small crowd gathered and stood outside the circle, unsure what this was all about. They may have wondered, "If this is a band, why don't they have matching shirts and why is everyone playing a different song?" Those in the circle invited others to play, but most people declined the offer of an instrument and moved quickly away. Co-workers from the *Kenosha News* avoided eye contact with me and walked on. We were undeterred by the response. We just kept playing—playing with whoever dropped by. By the end of the first hour, I had forgotten to worry about what anyone thought and had begun to use what has since become my favorite community drum circle cry, "Kids of all ages! No experience necessary!" When Howard Brown, then-publisher of the *Kenosha News*, passed by I smiled and promptly handed him one of our shakers made from a copper toilet float filled with popcorn.

After two hours in the sun we discovered that, yes, this was something new for our community but, yes, it was worth trying. I had taken a chance—of not knowing my stuff, of looking like a certifiable goofball in front of professional colleagues—and the chance had been worth it. We had put it out there for those who had never seen such a thing before. As a bonus, connections were made with people who would eventually come drum with us at our home circles.

We also discovered that many think drumming is for kids only. Although our adult drummer friends had joined us that day, nearly everyone else who ventured into the circle was a child under the age of 12. Some of the children were obviously there because an adult had pointed our way and said, "Why don't you go over and try that; it looks like fun." Some of these adults stood behind the chairs of their children but would not take an instrument; others parked their kids in the circle and went off in search of a beer.

Adults who embrace the drum circle's magic may not relate to this "just for kids" attitude. It's fairly understandable, however. It may look like drumming a kid thing because young children are often the most willing to engage in the unknown. Fearless and curious, they see the drums and percussion instruments as great new toys to be explored. The *serious adult* reaction to this is, "Sure, it's a good way to keep the kiddies busy, but it's not something *I* want to be seen doing in public."

I encountered this attitude again and again as I began to facilitate public drum circles. In July 2001 and 2002 I conducted drum circles at the Racine County Fair. Although my circle was billed as an all-ages activity at the Children's stage, on both occasions it wound up looking more like a babysitting drop-off point than an opportunity for music making. More than once during the events, I turned around to find myself ankle-deep in two-year-olds swinging away at my drums with sticks with no responsible adults in sight.

It *is* wonderful for children to play these instruments, but it is an experience that is enhanced when they have adults supporting their efforts and playing along with them. Adults who make the effort are rewarded by discovering that drumming is fun for them too and not just for their kids. For the kids it is a great opportunity to see their parents having fun and learning something new just like they are.

The second of this chapter's revelations is that drum circles do not have to consist only of drums. In fact, the best-sounding drum songs are those that include a wide range of musical voices—wood clackers, bells, cedar flutes and five-gallon water jugs.

In any given drum circle or drum class, children tend to be the first to experiment with non-drum instruments. As noted, children are the ones with the greatest sense of adventure (and sometimes the briefest attention spans) so they most often embrace opportunities for variety.

Conversely, some adult drum students are of a drum-only mindset. Many beginner drummers play the drum because that is what they truly love. Other adult drummers do not want to try new a percussion voice until they have mastered the drum. When I first began drumming I was not secure enough to put down my drum for an unknown entity like a set of clave sticks. Eventually I felt comfortable enough with my drum to experiment with the rhythm-making potential of a wider range of instruments.

In a community drum circle at which there are people who have not previously played a drum, another dynamic may be at work. Here, there may be adults who are intimidated by the invitation to play a drum but might be inclined to gently shake a tambourine or Easter egg filled with beach pebbles. Drum circle hosts, whose job is to maximize enjoyment of the drum circle experience, should always offer a wide range of percussion toys whether at home or out in the community. The intention is for drum circle songs to become a musical tapestry created from the sound threads of various instruments. Or, to use a food analogy, "A good community drum song is like well seasoned soup—drums are the meat and potatoes and percussion toys like shakers and bells are the special herbs and spices."

When we open the door to non-drum instruments, other cool things usually come in, particularly exotic instruments from other lands. Not long after a person begins drumming on an ethnic drum, he or she may be drawn to learn about and play other percussion instruments. I believe this is in part because the hand drums we start with come from indigenous peoples, cultures rich in tradition—musical and otherwise. It is hard to "just play an African drum" and not want to know about the people who made it, why they made it and what other instruments they may have played along with it. From this place, a novice djembe player may soon end up with a collection that includes a gourd scraper called a *guiro*, a double bell called a *gankogui*, a pair of clave sticks and a bead-covered gourd known as a *shekere*.

As this drummer discovers new instruments, he or she may attend drum circles featuring an even wider array of exotic music making items. Curiosity may then blossom to other cultures and their drums and their percussion toys and our hypothetical drummer is now checking out workshops on how to make a cedar flute or play the Brazilian *berimbau*!

This is the journey taken by Roger and me and many of those in our drum circle community. Although most of us began as students of the African drum, a few found our primary voice was actually something else—Middle Eastern tabla, Irish bodhran, or even a simple red tambourine. Some, like Ed Wozniak, have become adept in carving flutes or, like Tom Anger, who fashions didjeridus from plastic pipe with a blowtorch.

Down Under fun! In the author's basement, several play Australian-style didgeridus using five-gallon buckets for amplification. From left, Joy Wolf, Tom Anger, Tom Gill, John Von Eiff and Shirley Yanasek. Only Tom Gill's instrument is from Australian wood. Joy's is a cactus branch and the others are made from PVC pipe.

In the early years we were curious about everything—we took workshops on ethnic instruments in Milwaukee, Chicago, Kansas City and Denver. When we met a teacher who had particularly impressed us, we asked him or her to come to our house to do a workshop. In one year we hosted experts in the frame drum, the didjeridu and the throat singing style of Tuva. And at each we had participation from at least 10 people—fairly impressive for the Kenosha-Racine area!

Not every new instrument becomes a regular part of our repertoire, of course. I, for one, enjoyed but chose not to pursue throat singing. I did continue study of the didjeridu, Japanese taiko drumming and blues harmonica. Roger rediscovered his love of the guitar and plays a rather snappy Middle Eastern style recorder.

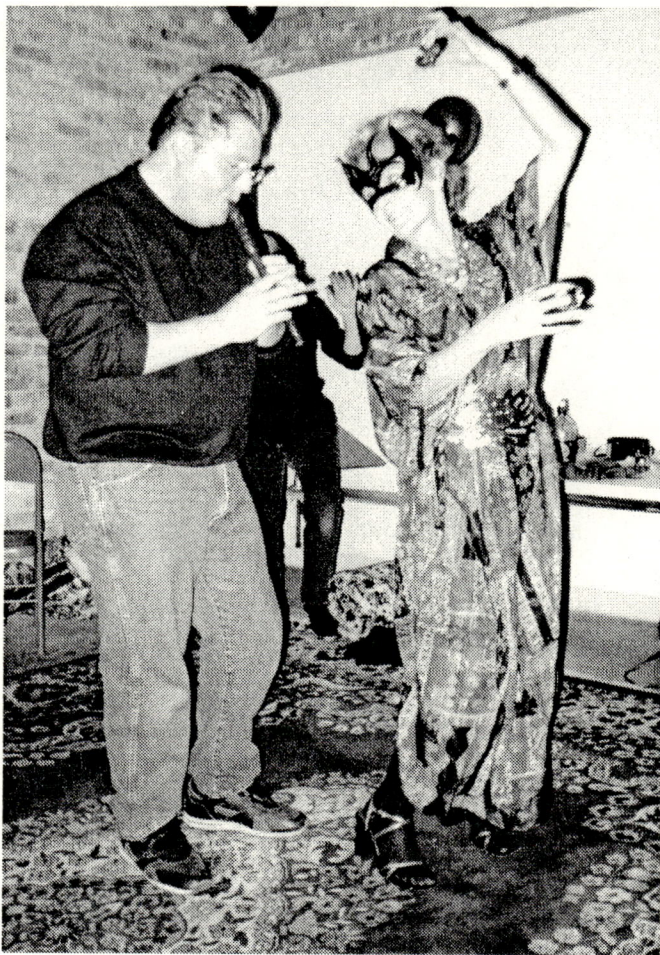

The very versatile Roger (costumed as a member of Blue Man Group) plays a Middle Eastern-style tune for dancer Sandy Bremer at Lemon Street Gallery's Mardi Gras party.

The "final frontier" of non-drum instruments is sometimes referred to as "Found Sound." In the event that we ever run out of cultures to musically investigate (and even if we don't), we have discovered there's a whole new world of percussion to be found in our kitchen cabinets and local hardware stores.

Found Sound is to percussion music as the collage is to traditional painting. The concept is that everything makes a sound when tapped, clacked or scrunched—all you have to do is add rhythm. STOMP and Blue Man Group are among the most famous to utilize Found Sound but most of us drum and percussion types eventually all begin exploring it. The exotic realm of Found Sound includes such non-instruments as Club-brand cast aluminum pot lids, crumpled plastic bags and picture wire plucked with a plastic comb. My personal favorite happens to be the five-gallon water bottle hit with a mallet made from blue jean material wrapped around a half-inch wooden dowel.

One Thanksgiving afternoon, Roger and I were standing around the kitchen with nothing much to do but watch the oven as the turkey roasted when we decided to make some music. At hand was a sink of clean dishes. I clinked a glass with a chopstick; he bonked a pan with a spoon. From glass to stainless sink to plastic cup—soon we had a fine multi-part rhythm.

What makes Found Sound a hit is the Fun Factor. Drummers and other musical types can get to a place where they take their instruments too seriously. They may also get into a rut with their favorite rhythms or songs. Making music with odd items puts the *play* back into *playing music*.

When rhythm facilitators go to community events, we like to demonstrate some of our favorite homemade instruments of the Found Sound variety. In addition to showing people how to add diversity to their drum sounds, it's a great way to show folks they don't have to have $250 for a drum to get started making music. Holding up a 99-cent paint bucket and a homemade mallet, I like to ask, "How much fun can you have for a dollar?"

Drum circle facilitators need to help the public recognize that drum culture is many things they might not have expected. It is kids, but it is also adults; it is drums, and also other percussion, other cultures and even unconventional instruments. If we love this music and the community circle, then as facilitators we must also facilitate an awareness of drum circle magic in all its manifestations.

Chapter 14

Recognizing Our Worth

Somewhere between thinking it was cool to share drums with others and hauling around enough equipment for 60 people, I discovered: even though I believe with all my heart that drumming is a good thing and I want to share this goodness with the world, there's a point at which you have to start asking tough questions. These questions are not, "How can I get 150 instruments by next Tuesday?" or "What do I do if I get lost in the fog at night on a winding country road on my way to a gig?" The really big questions come from the touchy subject of *money*. When people ask us to bring some drums to an event, we have to consider the fact that sometimes we need to ask for money in return. Sometimes we don't. And if we do, questions then include "For which events do we ask for money?" and "How much?"

Money is a tough one because it is very hard to put a price on what we do. A drum circle is not a consumer product. It is a service, but one that is challenging to define. A drum circle experience can be some or all of the following:

- Creative
- Educational
- Therapeutic
- Energizing
- Relaxing
- Fun

To quote a phrase used by Tom Gill, "We are not selling widgets here."

One of the interesting problems is that what we do does not translate well on paper. People in charge of "buying a drum circle experience" want to know what they're getting for their money. These people may never have sat in a drum circle and may not know what it sounds, looks or feels like. To them, $150 for an hour's drum circle can sound outrageous unless they understand what exactly goes into the creation of a drum circle event.

What does it take to *make* a drum circle? First there's a lot of *stuff*.

We're not like the guy who shows up with a guitar and his favorite sheet music or the clown who shapes balloons into animals—we bring enough things for everyone to play with at the same time. This means a lot of big drum things and many small hand held percussion items.

Also top of the list of circle facilitator requirements are physical strength and emotional flexibility. Specifically, a drum circle event begins by moving many rather large drums (some weighing up to 20 pounds), stacks of plastic buckets, baskets of percussion instruments (bells, shakers, clave sticks, mallets) and Tupperware™ containers of tambourines and frame drums from a storage point into a vehicle. These things are driven to a location where they are unloaded and taken to the drum circle venue and placed around the circle. The facilitator then facilitates the event, counts and collects the instruments, reloads his or her vehicle and returns home. There, the instruments are all unloaded and re-stored to their rightful places.

Ready to rock and roll—the author's Toyota Sienna van packed for a big gig three hours' drive from Kenosha. License plate, not pictured, says, "We Drum." Bumper sticker at right reads, "Another Woman on Drums."

So for starters, you've got an enormous output of physical energy. Then, an analysis of the actual equipment involved reveals an outlay of a substantial amount of money for inventory. Even at $1 for each bucket, things add up quickly. And should a real drum get accidentally broken during the event, the facilitator is looking at repair or replacement costs easily reaching $100.

At this point, even those not familiar with drum circle events may appreciate the rationale behind a facilitator's financial requests. Then there's the next question: Knowing the intensity of the labor involved, why would anybody consider becoming a drum circle facilitator in the first place?

Coming full circle—of course—we choose this path because we have found it is more fun when we drum with others than by ourselves. What we have to offer goes beyond the stuff we bring—it is the intangible commodity I can only describe as "goodness." We enjoy fostering the type of group unity that takes place during rhythm circle events. We appreciate comments like the one from a Cub Scout leader who told me, "We were going to hire a magician but I thought the boys needed something that was interactive and hands-on." And the observation made by a 17-year-old at a juvenile detention facility, "It's better to beat on drums than on each other."

To generate this unique type of magic, we have to have *stuff*. We love this stuff—the drums that ignited our percussive passion, even if they weigh a lot and take time and care to move around. Some of us refer to the hauling of our drums as "schlepping"—borrowed from the Yiddish word, "schlep." Even those at the top of this game find themselves schlepping equipment from place to place. Leaving a "Unity With A Beat!" weekend in Colorado (June 2001), I came across Arthur Hull sealing several large boxes of his drums with a tape gun. Looking up, he said, "Superstar—Roadie."

Understanding what goes into a drum circle begs another question, "When *don't* you ask for money?" There are times and reasons to give this away. New facilitators sometimes donate their time and talent because they know they have a lot to learn about leading drum circles. Experienced facilitators know they have something to offer that is worth paying for.

Other times it is just a labor of love. When I first started out I explored the possibility of sharing a drum experience with a group of developmentally disabled adults in Kenosha. This facility provided day programs for adults with mixed abilities—some independent in the community, others in need of constant care. Those on the more independent end of the spectrum reminded me of my sister Fraser, and so I hoped to share something I thought she would enjoy.

My first contact with agency staff was bittersweet. I was told I was welcome to bring in some drums but that money was a problem. When the site manager suggested he could "take $5 from the personal accounts of each of the clients" I decided the visit would be a freebie. How could anyone in good conscience take $5 from these people?

So sometimes you need to give it away. A few years ago, a medicine woman friend helped me to put things in perspective. She said, "I charge for my artwork but I do not charge for my medicine." To me drumming is a type of good medicine—there are times when it needs to be given away.

The tradition of the give-away has roots in Native American and other indigenous cultures. It is believed that a gift has more value to the receiver than it would have had it been kept by the giver. When deemed necessary, we do not put a price tag on our drum work. There's a time to charge, a time to give away. It's all about exchange and balance.

Rhythm in the Round, like many other drum circle communities, gave away time and space long before it asked for anything in return. Each month for the past four years Roger and I have offered a space in our house for a drum circle. We do not and never will ask for any sort of money or donation for these circles. This is because first, we can afford to do this, and second, we want to. We can afford to offer the space because it is neither a commercial storefront nor a facility we have to rent. We also believe that just by showing up people are giving gifts of rhythm and energy that benefit us all. How can you put a price on that?

To help us strike a balance between giving away free things and charging when appropriate, Rhythm in the Round became a home-based business. We worked up a striking logo and with help from Tom Gill (who also owns a graphic arts business) got some snazzy business cards, t-shirts and egg-shaped shakers with this logo imprinted on them.

In an ideal world, a drum circle organization generates enough paid gigs to balance giving others away when needed. In its early years, Rhythm in the Round has been mostly a hobby that pays for itself rather than a serious business. When it comes to promoting what we do we are not as enterprising as other drum circle organizations. Although I am aware that what we offer is unique and there is plenty of room for friendly competition among facilitators, I still struggle with the concept of presenting what we do to the broader community.

Challenges in the area of promoting Rhythm in the Round seem to be three-fold: a lack of extra time; some residual shyness on my part; and experience with the news media. The last of these, regarding the media, merits brief discussion. For nearly 14 years I handled requests from hundreds of community groups and agencies vying for free space in the newspaper. When Rhythm in the Round came into being, I did not want be one of those groups. I felt (maybe erroneously) that Rhythm in the Round should attract attention on its own merit—because it is cool and a unique asset to the Kenosha area—not because I begged for recognition. As of this writing this has not proven to be the case. *Kenosha News* reporters and photographers have attended our public circles, notebooks and cameras in hand, yet no story or photo has been published. (We have, however, had coverage in the *Milwaukee Journal-Sentinel*.) Maybe it's time for Rhythm in the Round to barter for the services of a business manager or public relations consultant.

Lack of publicity has not slowed us down, however. Each year I find myself being asked to conduct several drum circles a month—enough to make an interesting change from substitute teaching. Some have become regular events, such as the monthly circle at St. Joseph's adult day care and a community circle at the annual bicycle races.

These circles are a mix of well-paid, break-even and give-away events. One of our favorite freebies is really barter—"WomanSpirit Faire & Bizarre" in Racine, Wisconsin. On the first Sunday in May each year, we are asked to facilitate short drum circles to help kick off and close down this daylong gathering of artists, folk dancers, vendors and tarot card readers, sponsored by the women's group of the Olympia Brown Unitarian Universalist Church. In exchange for rallying the crowd, we are given a table at which to exhibit drums for sale and to hand out literature about our drum circles and lessons. Mostly, we sit at our table between drum circles chatting with drum circle pals and making new friends involved in art and music. Now that's fair trade!

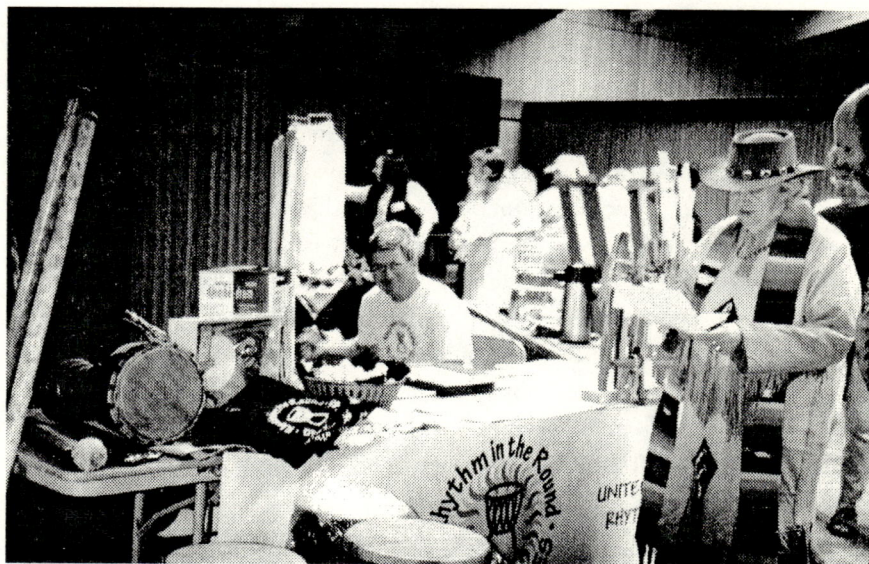

John Von Eiff watches the store at "WomanSpirit Faire & Bizarre," Racine, May 2003.

Rhythm in the Round and Tom's Rhythm for Unity are businesses *and* communities. Those who support us by drumming at public events like parades are given things in return such as picnic lunches and colorful t-shirts. Offering space, hospitality and egg shakers to fellow drummers fits well with the tradition of the give-away. It is also, in native tradition, good medicine.

After four years as a facilitator, I still strive to strike a balance between asking for money and giving freely of my time and energy. My personal sliding scale takes into account the type of group to whom I offer my services. Is it a large corporation with a healthy profit margin? Is it a camp with a built-in overhead for fun activities or a philanthropic organization, serving children with muscular dystrophy? It is hard to decide what and when to charge; and even money doesn't cover it all. To paraphrase an old recruitment slogan used by the armed forces, "It's the hardest job you'll ever love."

Even those who have been involved with drums and groups for some time wrestle with the question of reimbursement. Some may say they have a carved-in-stone "fee schedule," but if the cause is compelling enough, there's a good chance the facilitator or teacher will consider payment on a sliding scale. One of my models for this is Ubaka Hill. Ubaka conducts drumming workshops all over the world all year long. One of her missions is to encourage women to discover their power and voice through drumming. To this end Hill's workshops are often offered up at a suggested cost rather than a set fee.

Those at top dollar in the drum circle business might even admit that it's not all gravy—$700 for an event doesn't come to much after you factor in the cost of hundreds of instruments, pay several people to help you move the instruments and the hours of travel, set up and break down involved. When all is said and done, I believe many rhythm facilitators would agree it's not as much about the money as it is about the magic.

Chapter 15

Magic, Magic, Everywhere

> Magic is not the same as illusion—magic
> is real.
> —Heather Larson Poyner

Magic may be intangible and often unexplainable, but it *is* real. Magic is the burst of laughter from a man in a wheelchair clutching a tambourine with crippled hands. Magic is also:

- A blind woman named Tommy clapping pot lids together in 6/8 time.
- Adults recognizing the importance of play in their lives.
- Being invited into people's lives to help mark life passages of birth, graduation, marriage and even death.

Sometimes the magic shows up in the words of those who have been touched by exposure to the drums and the music we create together.

> I am thrilled to be here. I am pushing 97
> and when I play the drum, I know I'm
> still alive.
> —Nell,
> St. Joe's adult daycare, Kenosha

> I've been working (with developmentally
> disabled adults) for the past couple
> years and I have a sense—I'm not sure
> what—but that rhythmic sounds are very
> soothing to some of these people...do you
> think I'm onto something?
> —Lynn Otto,
> Career Industries, Racine, Wis.

These types of magic take place through a combination of energy of the drums, the spirit of those in the circle and sometimes the delicate guidance of a facilitator. The result is what I call "musical alchemy." One

103

of the definitions of "alchemy" is "mingling." It comes from the Greek word referring to the ancient concept of chemistry, which relied on the extraction of plant essences for medicine. Webster's Collegiate Dictionary (my edition is circa 1945) notes that in medieval times the purpose of alchemy was "to transmute base metals into gold and discover the universal cure for diseases and means of indefinitely prolonging life."

Consider now the role of rhythm facilitator. He or she takes a collection of instruments to a group of people who may not have previously played the instruments. The facilitator then helps foster bonds of camaraderie and generates a joy for music making. The rhythm facilitator seems very much like the alchemist, with the exception that he or she is capable of producing gold nearly every time.

Magic is also the word that describes amazing coincidences that have taken place since drums came into our lives. There have been many, but a few highlights are in order.

In June 1998, two years before we discovered drumming, my father received a hand drum for his birthday. My stepmother, Stella, decided to buy him a drum called an *ashiko* from a man who crafted drums in their town of Eureka Springs, Arkansas. Up to that time, with the exception of my great aunt Katherine, a piano teacher, no one in my family had played a musical instrument, much less a drum. Hearing that Stella had procured a drum with a tie-dyed head had a strange effect on me. "My dad got a drum for his birthday!" I thought excitedly. I had never set eyes on a hand drum, but I was, for some reason, really happy that he had gotten one.

In the summer of 2001, Roger and I visited my parents and brought along some of our newly acquired drums and percussion instruments. Although my dad told us he had no rhythm, it wasn't long before the four of us were creating fine in-the-moment music together. On our next visit, my dad arranged for us to conduct a drum circle in downtown Eureka Springs and arranged for our photo to appear in the local paper.

Left, the author's father, Read Larson, explores rhythms on his ashiko in 2001. His wife, Stella, also plays an ashiko.

Another magic-tinged coincidence occurred when Roger and I took a workshop on the art of playing the didjeridu. This is a horn-like instrument first used by the ancient Aborigines of Australia. They discovered that blowing into a tree branch that had been hollowed out by termites produced powerful droning vibrations with layers of harmonic sound. They used the instrument in male initiation rites and to invoke trance and an alternate reality known as the Dreamtime. During the workshop, 10 participants blowing into didjeridus produced a lot of strong vibrations. Long story short, halfway through the workshop my watch stopped. As we left for home, it started up again on its own.

Another synchronicity occurred in autumn 2004. On Oct. 2, I was scheduled to lead a drum workshop at The Synchronicity Learning Center, Burlington, Wisconsin. After I had accepted the job, a friend asked Roger and I to provide drumming for an event in Chicago showcasing the artwork of an exiled Tibetan monk, also slated for Oct. 2. Roger, who had not yet soloed a circle, said he would do it. At the last minute, however, my class was cancelled so we both loaded up the van and headed to Chicago.

The moment we set foot in the building (a former funeral home turned yoga studio) Roger and I felt out of our depth. Crowded into a narrow hallway were well-dressed people sipping chai tea watching two scantily clad women perform modern dance. The honored guest, the monk, attired in traditional scarlet silk robe and prayer beads, glided through the room. Roger and I stood in the doorway with a cartful of African drums wearing our Rhythm in the Round t-shirts. At best we felt "out of sync."

Then, as we waited to do our drum circle thing, the monk, Romio Shrestha, addressed the group. He did not begin with a presentation of his artwork, or a plea for those attending to donate money to alleviate the suffering of his brother monks, but softly spoke of things that mattered most to him: compassion, divinity within each person, and his personal quest for 1,000 goddesses and the White Tara. When asked about China's repression of Tibetan culture, Romio gently replied, "Such things are only material, I came to address the eternal."

I might not have followed his entire discourse on Buddhist perspective, but Romio's intent was accomplished. His words melted away differences and ego, and I knew Roger and I could and should offer a drum circle to this group. Still, it wasn't going to be easy. Coming at the tail end of the evening, the crowd thinned and the circle began with several tired, restless five-year-olds. I thought about offering up some profound words, but everything important had already been said. Instead, Roger and I worked to rein in the wild energy of the children and help adults enter the song. Within a few minutes, the monk joined us, picked up a frame drum and played along.

At the end of our allotted time, we packed up to leave. When we got to our van we realized we had left something behind. I volunteered to retrieve it because I felt I needed to say goodbye to the monk. One of the evening's hostesses thanked me for our drum circle and Romio took my hand in both of his and looked at me steadily. He said he greatly enjoyed the drumming circle. "It was pure magic," he said. Validation vibrated through me—clear as a temple bell, resonant as a Tibetan bowl.

Call it coincidence or synchronicity or just being in the right place at the right time. The more I connect to drums, the more such things seem to happen. I am convinced there is an undeniable connection between the drum circle, the classroom and my family circle.

Barely one month before this manuscript was completed, I had another coincidental experience—an interesting discovery regarding ancestors on my father's side of the family. Visiting Dad at Easter 2005, I was given papers tracing several generations of Larsons. It seems that during the 1850s my great great-grandfather, Gustave May, had been the proprietor of two dining establishments and one hotel in downtown Chicago. This fascinated me, as one of my early dreams was to own a restaurant. This could explain why today I do what I do with drum circles—I've got a "hospitality gene"!

Another area of magical impact has been the effect of drums on our immediate family. Our children are now in their teenage years, the crossroads of childhood and adulthood. They can choose to disown us or embrace us. Ours are walking a path somewhere in between. Lauren has come to drumming workshops, acted as my co-facilitator and dabbled with the cedar flute. She has decided drumming is not for her (she sings) but says drums have made me more fun as mothers go.

Alex, who was once very sound sensitive and not fond of strangers in his home, has discovered some of our drum friends are now his friends, too. Although he may be a tad self-conscious when his mother shows up at his school with a cartload of drums to put on a program for his classmates, I believe that he is secretly sort of proud of me.

Now age 13, Alex has begun music exploration of his own. A year ago he listened to movie sound tracks. This year he spent his birthday money to buy classical music CDs with titles like *The World's Great Piano Concertos*. He is also a beginner level trumpet player with music-reading ability that far exceeds that of his parents.

Preparing this book, I was thinking about contacting a former drum student to tell him I was planning to include his photo. Robert had been the only student to complete a rainstick project at the Boys and Girls Club way back in the autumn of 2000. Just as I wondered how to reach him, he appeared as one of my students in a school where I was substitute teaching.

It had been four years since he had seen me but Robert remembered our drum and rainstick class and began tapping out "Mama Pappa" on his desktop.

Robert and his rainstick: the magic of pride in a job well done.

I believe all of these kinds of coincidences and revelations remind us to keep looking through our windows of awareness for opportunities to connect with one another.

To round out this chapter of magic, I leave you with a dream. It is a dream I had a long, long time ago—shortly after talking with Tom Gill about drums but before actually hearing or attending a drum circle. The following is an excerpt from the journal I was keeping at the time:

Dec. 12, 1999

Catching the beat

Coincidences, dreams and
revelations through the drum…
which I do not own physically…
maybe it owns me in spirit?

Last night I dreamt of a drum
circle. I had joined it as it was in
progress and it was almost over.
The participants seemed reluctant
to play with an outsider present.
One woman started to tap the
drum at her side (a short brown
drum with a small head). Another
woman showed me what was inside
her drumhead (it seemed natural to
me that the drum could be opened
up). Inside was a treasure of
gems—uncut stones that seemed
to be lapis lazuli with speckled gold
edges and possibly also quartz
crystals.

The images, literal and metaphorical, speak volumes. Through whatever vehicle we choose to name it—convergence, coincidence or heightened perception, I was given a preview of this journey—yes, potential obstacles, but even more, treasures beyond price.

During these first years we have encountered fear, apprehension and even resentment from some who question our choice to offer hand drums in a community setting. But for every person who has said, "Don't go there," there have been many more who say, "Tell me more!" and "Bring it on!" These are the uncut stones, the diamonds in the rough, revealed in the head of that woman's drum. Each of us is indeed an uncut gem, brought to brilliance as we sit and share our musical, magical gifts in the community drum circle.

Epilogue

New Year's Day at the lakefront; a basement full of drums. Looking around my house and at my life today I cannot imagine what it would have been like had the drums not found me five-plus years ago. My daily life and the lives of those in my family circle now vibrate at a different frequency. Nearly every room in our physical home has been influenced in some way by a new cultural awareness—from Monne Haug's horn-adorned mask in our living room to the prehistoric cave theme created on our kitchen walls by Roger, Lauren and myself using our handprints dipped in terra cotta colored paint.

The author strikes a drum-inspired pose in her strikingly decorated kitchen, spring 2005.

The job I do for a living has changed, as has how and with whom our family celebrates annual holidays. Even the outgoing message on our answering machine has the touch of the drum—would-be callers find themselves greeted by rhythm and blues guitar, Middle Eastern flute and tambourine or Native American powwow drums.

Best of all, our formerly small family has many new members. Without the drum to draw community to our doors, Roger and I never would have made contact with the dozens of wonderful people we now know—artists, storytellers, teachers and massage therapists, to name a few.

On Sunday, Oct. 13, 2004, Gary Green, priest of St. Andrew's Episcopal Church, asked the congregation, "Looking back five years would your life today be what you expected?"

I am not sure *what* it would have been, but it probably wouldn't have been *this*. The question is, "Why?" Why these changes, shifts in perception, vocation and home decoration? I believe things were set in motion five years ago not just so that Roger and I could have a little more icing on the cake of our personal lives, but so we could have a positive impact on the lives of those around us.

This positive impact has taken the form of introducing drum circle gatherings to people who had never before experienced them. And we chose to do this not just because it made us feel good, but because we realized it made other people feel good, too. Every time I add a new name to our mailing list of 80-plus, I wonder what new connections this person will make or friends he or she will meet by attending one of the drum events in our newsletter.

As this story comes to an end, I find I am still writing notes in a spiral notebook, and I'm still chasing this elusive thing called *magic*. Recurrent throughout this journey has been the discovery that I have tapped into something much needed in the world today.

That *something* is the desire to unplug from our technology and connect with our humanity. In March 2001, I wrote:

> It's not just me—drumming is
> everywhere...the thirst, the hunger,
> passion is not mine alone, it is in
> the hearts of many people of many
> ages and populations.

There are many ways to feed those hungry for a drumming experience. Our particular path has been affirmed time and again, and as recently as two months ago, as I was finishing this manuscript. It happened as Doug Wile, an experienced conga player from New York City, told a group of drum workshop participants at Tom Gill's about the drum scene in the Big Apple. "Street corners throughout New York City are alive with the talents of drummers from around the world," Doug began. "However, these drummers do not allow outsiders into their inner circle," he said.

"The music scene (in New York) is very exclusive," Doug said. "When I came to Wisconsin and Tom's place, I was impressed by the inclusive nature of what he offers here. There is nothing like this in New York City. Tom offers drum circles that are inclusive, not exclusive."

For Tom, and those of us who aspire to this model, it doesn't get any more validating than this.

The key, the beauty, and yes, maybe even the magic here is the *inclusive* nature of the drum circle experience. A reflection from spring, 2001, as people began to find their way to our living room drum circle:

> Historically in the West, people
> have been entertained by music,
> content to go to concerts and the
> symphony...music to be enjoyed
> passively. What's happening now:
> We no longer go to the symphony,
> we are the symphony. Everybody,
> everywhere, all together. No one
> left out, no one on the sidelines.
>
> —"Spiral Series IV,"
> March 17, 2001

It turns out that our role is to help people find their way into this symphony of souls.

Roger and I began drum circles here in Kenosha because it seemed like a good idea at the time. We recently learned however, that drum circles might be more important to our community than we could have possibly imagined. In late 2004, a report titled "Sperlings Best Places" published statistics ranking the quality of life in many towns and cities. Of the 117 "most stressful small cities in America," *Kenosha* came in ninth. Assessed factors included jobs lost due to factory closings and long commutes to work in Chicago and Milwaukee. I wonder, however, if "quality of life" is also perhaps a factor. There are plans to open a casino here, but personally I don't see a casino as a tool for community stress reduction.

Kenosha is far from alone when it comes to stress today. In communities throughout the planet people are stressed out from the threat of war and the reality of unemployment and disease; depersonalization in the workplace and over-reliance on pharmaceuticals.

Roger and I think that in some small way we are improving the quality of life in our community. We know, at the very least, that we have made an impact on the lives of some people. This message was brought home to us in September 2004 at a gathering of musicians. When we arrived for the all-day event at Southport Beach House, we discovered a diverse group—members of the Celtic Strings, an Irish band from Racine; students of African drumming; and masters of the Native American cedar flute.

John Bloner, event host, invited participants to share their "musical odyssey" with the group. Quite a few noted they had attended our drum circles or gotten involved in ethnic music because they had met us. There were people who had marched with us in parades, drummers we had met at Tom Gill's and a woman named Carolyn, there because she had heard us at Hawthorne Hollow and said drums had helped change her life. Many wore Rhythm in the Round shirts.

Some people think they are starting to see positive changes in Kenosha. One is Ron Larson (no known relation to the author), who has attended our home circles. Ron, a native of Kenosha, spent several years studying in California. Returning home, Ron discovered us as we were drumming by the lake on New Year's Day 2002. Ron observed that the presence of things like Lemon Street Art Gallery and Rhythm in the Round point to a kind of "Kenosha Renaissance."

To keep things in perspective Roger and I and other facilitators must remember that community building is more about roots than roles. In the words of Malidoma Patrice Somé:

> A chief is only a keeper of a particular power
> that people respect deeply…in a sense, a chief
> is not a chief; a chief is a person who happens to
> bring a particular set of gifts to the community.

114

For my part I have to bear in mind that not everyone is as excited about this calling as I am. Not everyone, including the co-founders of Rhythm in the Round, waits for the phone to ring with a request to drive 100 drums to a Boy Scout Meeting or spends hours making a homemade drum from packing tape and 12-inch boards.

In his homily Gary Green also observed that our life journeys are about "perseverance and integrity" and sometimes "just showing up." The bottom line, he said that day, is to ask ourselves the ultimate question, "How can we be of greater service…to the community?"

I know drumming cannot solve the world's worst crises. But healing can begin with our own small circle. Maybe this is why: "Why me?" "Why us?" "Why here?" and "Why now?".

The people of our communities—Kenosha and beyond—need meaningful ways to connect to one another. It's not hard if you believe in magic. We need to believe that the magic of meaningful connection is possible. Drum circles are one place to find magic, but we also need to be on the lookout for magic everywhere in everyday life. As Mickey Hart points out: "magic won't happen unless you set a place at the table for it."

I am just one of many called to facilitate the magic of connection. The tools at hand are the drums in our hands. And hope, like the circle where we gather, is boundless.

Namaste,

Heather

Why here, why us. Rhythm in the Round drummers happy but tired at the end of the Civic Veteran's Parade, June 2002.

About the Author

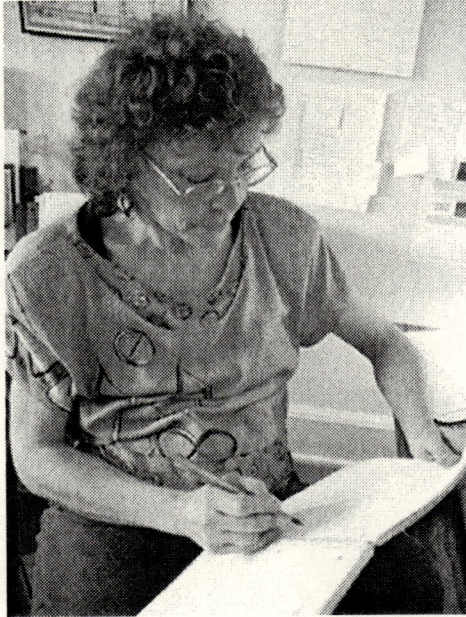

Heather Larson Poyner was born in 1957 in White Plains, N.Y. Curiosity and a fascination with words resulted in a degree in journalism from the University of Wisconsin-Madison in 1979.

Heather wrote and edited Advance Magazine for the Episcopal Diocese of Chicago. She married Roger Poyner in 1987.

Seeking green space and better parking the Poyners moved to Kenosha, Wis., in 1989. Heather began working for the Kenosha News as a features reporter. Heather discovered hand drums in 2000 and in 2003 quit the News to pursue an almost-forgotten desire to teach and newfound love of leading drum circles.

Heather and Roger live in Kenosha with their children Lauren and Alexander and a basement full of drums.

Printed in the United States
39271LVS00006B/49-147